W9-CCQ-947

The Passion and Death of Jesus

John P. Gilbert

ABINGDON PRESS
Nashville

THE PASSION AND DEATH OF JESUS

by John P. Gilbert

Copyright © 2000 by Abingdon Press. All Rights Reserved.

No part of this work may be reproduced or transmitted in any form or by any means, electronic or mechanical, including photocopying and recording, or by any information storage or retrieval system, except as may be expressly permitted by the 1976 Copyright Act or in writing from the publisher. Requests for permission should be addressed to Abingdon Press, 201 Eighth Avenue South, P. O. Box 801, Nashville, Tennessee 37202-0801 or faxed to 615-749-6512.

This book is printed on recycled, acid-free paper.

Scripture quotations, unless other indicated, are from the New Revised Standard Version of the Bible, copyright © 1989, by the Division of Christian Education of the National Council of the Churches of Christ in the United States of America, and are used by permission. All rights reserved.

ISBN 0-687-09069-5

04 05 06 07 08 09—10 9 8 7 6 5

MANUFACTURED IN THE UNITED STATES OF AMERICA

Contents

Meet the Writer

John P. "Jack" Gilbert, a pastor, Christian educator, and Bible study author, with his wife, Nan Zoller, are the co-pastors of a small-membership congregation in rural Tennessee. Prior to his present appointment, Jack served the church for twenty-eight years through curriculum resource development, promotion, and sales as a staff member of The United Methodist Publishing House.

A graduate of the University of Minnesota and Boston University School of Theology, Jack has undertaken graduate work in religious education at Boston University and at several other universities and seminaries. His passions are adult Christian education, the local congregation, and the Gospel of John (although not necessarily in that order).

Jack and Nan are the parents of five grown children and the grandparents of six-year-old Jake, from whom Jack and Nan are learning to see the world God created with new wonder and joy.

A Word of Welcome

Welcome to THE PASSION AND DEATH OF JESUS, a study of the events of Holy Week. This study will allow you to walk with Jesus through the last days of his life and to take a close look at what happened, day by day, from his predictions of his death to the Crucifixion. Here you will find

- An examination of the three predictions of the Passion, the disciples' reaction to those predictions, and why Jesus resolved to go to Jerusalem, knowing it would lead to trouble;
- The forces of opposition to Jesus, the political scene in Rome, and the religious structures of the day;
- A Holy Week chronology, including background on the Passover; Jesus' "cleansing" of the Temple; the disciples' preparation for the Passover; the ritual foot-washing; and the prediction of Jesus' betrayal;
- Jesus' time of prayer in the garden of Gethsemane, a character portrayal of Judas, Jesus' encounter with the mob and his arrest, and the flight of the disciples to safety;
- The series of events at Jesus' trial before Caiaphas and some members of the Sanhedrin, Jesus' abuse at the hands of the religious and civil authorities, Jesus' encounter with Pilate, and other undercurrents that pushed events to their conclusion;
- The physical and political details about crucifixion and Jesus' traditional route to Golgotha, what happened specifically to the crucified Jesus, and his last words on the cross;
- The burial of Jesus, how to make meaning of what happened, how to understand the Atonement, and the events of Easter morning.

We invite you to delve deeply into this study of the Passion and death of Jesus and pray that you will find a blessing in it.

How to Use This Resource

We hope you enjoy participating in this study, either on your own or with a group. We offer these hints and suggestions to make your study a success.

THE PASSION AND DEATH OF JESUS is a self-contained study with all the teaching/learning suggestions conveniently located in the margin near the main text to which they refer. They are identified with the same heading (or a close abbreviation) as the heading in the main text. In addition to your Bible, all you need to have a successful group or individual study session is provided for you in this book.

Some special features are provided as well, such as the **Bible 301** activities in the teaching helps. We usually think of the "101" designation as the beginning level; these "301" designations prompt you to dig deeper. In these instances you will be invited to look up Scriptures, key words, or concepts in a Bible dictionary, commentary, or atlas. On occasion, an added book or resource is cited that may be obtained from your local library or perhaps from your pastor. Those resources are extras; your study will be enriched by these added sources of information, but it is not dependent on them.

This study is intentionally invitational. In the closing activity, you are invited to do three things: to give prayerful consideration to your relationship to Jesus Christ and make or renew your commitment, to offer your own spoken prayers, and to pray with and for others. We trust you will participate in these activities as you feel comfortable and that you will use them as a challenge to grow more confident with prayer and with your covenant with Jesus Christ.

Session One

Prediction and Resolve

Session Focus ◼
This session focuses on Jesus' understanding of who he was and what he felt he must do to fulfill God's calling, even though his closest supporters were confused and afraid.

Session Objective ◼
With thoughtful examination of the texts, you will come to a deeper understanding of and appreciation for the resolve Jesus had in facing the suffering and death he would ultimately endure.

Session Preparation ◼
If possible, obtain a copy of a Gospel parallel, a reference book that lines up together the passages from the Synoptic Gospels that are similar. Your pastor or church library may have a copy.

Choose from among these activities and discussion starters to plan your lesson.

How Do We Know? ◼
Without looking at your Bible, reconstruct as much of the events of Holy Week as you can. Jot down the

A man named Jesus (a common name of the time and a variation of *Joshua*), a carpenter from Nazareth in the Galilee, lived during the governorships of the Roman procurators in Palestine some two thousand years ago. He became a wandering preacher and teacher. He went to Jerusalem to celebrate the Passover and the Feast of Unleavened Bread; and while there, he was arrested, prosecuted, convicted, and executed by crucifixion. On the third day after the execution, he rose from the dead and appeared numerous times to his followers.

On these simple facts rests the faith of millions of persons across the globe. On these simple facts the course of the world's history has been changed time and again. On these simple facts, lives have been transformed, persons have been made new, and reality itself has been reoriented.

How Do We Know?

These facts are attested to in the Gospels, Epistles, and other writings in the Bible, the basic book of faith of those who seek to obey this man.

The facts are also attested to in non-Christian sources written during and shortly after the time of the man Jesus. The Roman historian Tacitus, for example, talks of *Christians*. He explains that their name comes

major events in order and then as many details about each event as you can remember. Keep your list posted throughout the study and add to it (and correct it, if necessary). Notice how much of what you have written is handed down from our religious tradition, how much is biblical, and how much the Gospels diverge from one another.

Does the reference to Jesus, Christ, or Christians in extra-biblical texts add any weight to the Bible's record of the Crucifixion and Resurrection for you? Explain.

from *Christ*, a man who, in the reign of Tiberius Caesar, was condemned to death by Pontius Pilate (Tacitus, *Annals*, 15, 44). Another Roman historian, Suetonius, writing in *Life of Claudius* (Chapter 25), makes mention of the belief of many in a crucified and risen Christ. Other historians of the first two centuries of the Common Era (A.D.) refer indirectly to the crucifixion and resurrection of the man Jesus, called the Christ. These historians and contemporary writers include among others such persons as the Romans Pliny the Younger and Celsus and the Jewish archivist Josephus.

But the primary record of the events leading up to the execution of Jesus by crucifixion and his resurrection on the third day is contained in the canonical Gospels of Matthew, Mark, Luke, and John. True, other writings and stories relate details of these events; but these other stories are noncanonical. That is to say, these are stories of Jesus that were not regarded as inspired, God-directed, and totally true by the great councils of the church that set the canon or contents of the Holy Scriptures. The first council took place at Nicea in A.D. 325 and dealt mainly with determining the boundaries of orthodoxy, that is, what was "official" Christian belief.

Thus, while acknowledging the existence of nonreligious references to the execution and resurrection of Jesus the Christ and the presence of noncanonical stories that relate dimensions and details of the execution and resurrection, our discussion will be limited to the descriptions of the events surrounding the Crucifixion in the canonical Gospels, those stories of Jesus that the church has regarded as true and God-inspired throughout the history of the Christian faith.

Problems With Sources ■

Form four teams. Choose any event from the Passion narrative, and then assign each group to look it up in one of the four Gospels.

What are the similarities in the story as told by the particular Gospel writer? What are the differences? Who is present in one account but missing in another? Does anyone do something different in one account than it was reported in another? Are there differences in the saying or action of Jesus among the four accounts?

If the event is missing from one or more of the Gospels, what does that suggest to you? Does the fact that there are differences among the texts matter to you? Explain.

Together, choose a noteworthy event from US or international history that occurred during the lifetime of the youngest member of the group. (Everyone needs to have some memory of it, even if as a young child.)

Tell them to "Write your own brief 'history' of that event. Choose the audience for whom your history is

The Problems With Sources

We cannot, however, simply take the Gospels in the New Testament at face value if we wish to understand in depth the execution and resurrection of Jesus. Several concerns about the Gospel accounts of the passion of Jesus are apparent immediately to anyone who reads the four accounts.

First, the Gospels are not consistent one with another. Each tells a slightly different story in which details vary. The four Gospels tell the same overall story, but they cannot be harmonized, that is, made congruent. The lack of consistency in sequence and detail among the four is evident to any reader.

Before the Gospels are impeached due to these inconsistencies, however, we must remember that the Gospel writers were not writing historical narratives nor were they writing biographies of the man Jesus. The Gospel writers were proclaiming their faith in the Word made flesh (John 1:1, 14); the Gospels are indeed the good news, news proclaimed loudly and clearly even though the details may not square one with another. The Gospels are theology; they are faith; they are not history in the sense that Josephus and Tacitus attempted to write history.

Second, did the Gospel writers fall prey to the same problems that historians face? History is always written after the fact and is therefore colored by the conditions or situations in which the historians find themselves. The present in which historians live can and almost always does alter their perceptions of the past about which they write. Even though the Gospel writers were not historians in the formal sense, did the times and locations in which they wrote affect their perceptions of the times of the man Jesus?

written (but don't reveal that until the discussion). Include at least the major figures, who did what to whom, what the most significant action or turning point was, who 'won' (if that is an issue), who was affected by the event and how."

Then compare the histories. How do the details vary? What prominence was given to certain details by one "historian" but not by another? Is there any variation in your histories because of varying age-related perceptions?

If the Gospel writers recorded their message so many years after the fact of Jesus' crucifixion and resurrection, might that account for variations in the text? What about the differences in audience? How did your own life experiences and values affect what you included and how you interpreted it? Could this sort of factor have influenced the Gospel writers as well?

Ask a volunteer to read aloud Matthew 24:29-31, then to read it again, then to read it a third time. Now ask another volunteer to recite it, exactly, without looking at the Bible. Invite anyone who wants to try to repeat these three verses verbatim. The original reader can keep track of the reciter's accuracy.

Consider one isolated example with reference to the Gospels: Scholars report that the Gospels were not written until as few as twenty and as many as seventy years after the resurrection of Jesus Christ. In the years between the Resurrection and the writing of the Gospels, many events took place that put the Gospel writers into realities quite different from that of the time of the execution of Jesus. During the latter part of the first century of the Common Era, Christians were struggling to gain acceptance by and within the Roman Empire on the one hand and had actively declared their independence from (and increasingly, rejection of) Jewish religion on the other hand.

As a consequence, the Gospels seem to place much of the blame for the execution of Jesus on the Jewish state while soft-pedaling the participation of Rome, especially Pontius Pilate, in that execution. In fact, Pilate comes across in the Gospels as weak, indecisive, and unsure of himself while Roman histories of the time present Pilate as ruthless, powerful, dogmatic, and decisive. So, is the picture of Pilate in the Gospels colored to reflect in part the attempt by Christianity to gain acceptance by Rome? Was deflecting some of the blame for the execution from Rome perhaps an unconscious attempt to make Christianity more tolerated within the Empire?

Third, a closely related issue concerning the sources are the words of Jesus used in the Gospels. Realistically, we must admit that no one followed Jesus with a tape recorder or with writing implements to record verbatim everything he said. If, as scholars tell us, the Gospels were written at least a generation after the Resurrection, can we assume that the words of Jesus in the

Could anyone do it, even after hearing it three times? Some persons learn best by verbal means: listening, reciting, memorizing; many learn best in several other ways. Was this easier for verbal learners? for participants from an oral culture? What does this simple exercise suggest about the potential of the Gospels to have recorded the *exact* words of Jesus, rather than the general idea and intent?

Do you believe that the Bible was divinely dictated by God? is a faithful recording of events, remembered as well as possible by the faithful writer(s)? was "inspired," but not dictated word for word by the mind of God? something else? How do the different understand-

Gospels are literally the actual words Jesus spoke in every case? Or do the reports of the words of Jesus in the Gospels, written in Greek, contain the core of what Jesus said while perhaps not being the precise words Jesus uttered in his Aramaic tongue?

Certainly, some of Jesus' words were so memorable that they were repeated and remembered in unwritten form for many years. But because some of his other words appear in more than one Gospel in slightly different forms, we may have to assume that some of the statements of Jesus as quoted in the Gospels may not be his *precise* words, even though they certainly convey the points he was trying to make.

A typical example of this is the similarity between the Sermon on the Mount in Matthew 5–7 and the Sermon on the Plain in Luke 6:20-49. Both recount the words of Jesus in slightly different ways, but both convey precisely the same meanings. Might the Gospel writers have remembered the words of Jesus, but forgotten the exact context in which he uttered some of these words? Might the Gospel writers have "read his words back into events" rather than knowing with certainty what words where uttered at which events? Or did Jesus preach the same sermon on more than one occasion (as contemporary preachers often do!)? If this were the case, why is this not mentioned in the Gospels?

If the Gospel writers did reflect in part the times in which they wrote and if the Gospel writers did rearrange somewhat the sequence of the statements of Jesus, what does this say about the inspiration of the Gospels? It says that the Gospel writers were clearly, profoundly, and unquestionably inspired by God, but that the Gospels were not "dictated" word

ings of the nature of the Scriptures affect how we read and understand it? How we accord it authority?

Consider also the questions raised here in the text.

by word by God. If God had dictated the four Gospels word by word, why are inconsistencies among the Gospels obvious? Would not God have dictated the four Gospels in the same way or at least with internal consistency? To think that God would have purposely dictated different details to different Gospel writers in order to confuse readers is a contradiction of much of the rest of the Scriptures, for example, Psalm 19:7b.

A fourth concern is the "source of the sources." Many scholars (but not all) argue that Mark was the first Gospel to be written and that Matthew in particular and Luke to a lesser extent rely heavily on Mark's Gospel. In fact, much of the Gospel of Mark is found in both Matthew and Luke. There is strong scholarly evidence for another source contemporary with Mark, known as "Q," (for *quelle*, German for "source") that was also used independently by Matthew and Luke.

John, on the other hand, presents a considerably different Gospel with little apparent "borrowing" from the other Gospels. This, among many other bits of evidence, has made many scholars contend that John was written considerably later than the three Synoptic Gospels, Matthew, Mark, and Luke. (The word *synoptic* means "sharing the same viewpoint or perspective.")

Bible 301 ☐

Using commentaries or a Bible dictionary, look up the introduction to Matthew, Mark, and Luke. What does the commentary say about the author? his audience? the sources of information used by the author? What is "Q," and what does that source add to the Gospel's records?

When the passion of Jesus is examined in the Gospels, however, the four Gospels are almost reduced to three. Matthew's account of the passion of Jesus relies very heavily on Mark's account; indeed, Matthew's account has been called an expansion of Mark's account. The expansions consist of blocks of teachings of Jesus inserted at various places in the sequence of events leading up to the Crucifixion.

As a consequence, scholars speak of the

How does this information on sources add to (or take from) your understanding and appreciation of the historical, theological, and devotional value of the Bible?

Matthew-Mark account of the Passion, Luke's account of the Passion, and John's account of the Passion, recognizing some variations in details among these three accounts. Which of the three (or four) is the most accurate? No one knows with certainty with regard to minor details.

But the recognition of the audiences for which the four Gospel writers wrote does shed some light on these variations. Matthew, for example, is thought to have written to convince Jews that Jesus was the fulfillment of the Old Testament prophecies. Luke, on the other hand, is addressed primarily to Gentile, that is, non-Jewish, readers. For example, Luke relies much less on relating Jesus to Old Testament prophecy than does Matthew. John, often conceded to be the last of the four written, was also aimed at a Gentile audience; for John reflects the times in which the Gospel writer lived, a time of increased antagonism between church and synagogue, between the Christians and the Jews.

Given these issues related to the sources of our knowledge of the execution and resurrection of Jesus, we can conclude for the purposes of this discussion that the Gospels are probably more consistent relative to the passion of Jesus than to many other dimensions of his life (for example, only Luke and Matthew tell stories of Jesus' birth, and these are quite dissimilar stories. See Matthew 1:18–2:15 and Luke 1–2).

Despite the possibility that the Gospel writers may have read some statements of Jesus back into the text and despite the fact that the Gospel writers may have reflected the times in which they wrote, we must accept the Gospels as they are at present. It is the Gospels in their present mode that have transformed the lives of many persons, and indeed the world, by telling their own story of Jesus the Christ.

Passion Beginnings

Passion Beginnings ■

Read Luke 2:22-38. What glimpses do you see in the words and actions of Simeon and Anna that this child Jesus was marked for his "ultimate destiny"?

Jesus, the Word become flesh (John 1:14), was, according to the Gospels, born for (or inexorably headed toward) an ultimate destiny of execution by crucifixion and resurrection. For example, Simeon, a "righteous and devout" man, recognized the infant Jesus at thirty-three days of age when the child was taken to the Temple (Luke 2:22-35). Simeon proclaimed that this infant was indeed the Messiah, but he also warned Mary that a "sword will pierce your own soul too," referring perhaps to Mary's witness of the execution of her son.

Read John 1–2. How does the Gospel of John introduce Jesus and his "ultimate destiny"? Do you think it was *necessary* that Jesus should have come into life in order to die in this way? Did God *plan and intend* that Jesus should become incarnate in order to be crucified? Explain your responses.

According to John's Gospel, Jesus himself was aware of the inevitable execution and resurrection very early in his ministry. Although the sequence of events here conflicts somewhat with the sequence in the Synoptic Gospels, John's Gospel reports Jesus announcing the execution and Resurrection as early as a few days, perhaps a week, after his own baptism by the hand of John. Note in John 1:29, John sees Jesus and speaks of him; John 1:43 reports on what Jesus did "the next day. . . ." John 2:1 then moves on to the next day and tells of the wedding in Cana of Galilee; and John 2:12 accounts for the next "few days" that Jesus spent with his mother, brothers, and disciples. Next, Jesus goes to Jerusalem for the Passover (John 2:13), enters the Temple and cleanses it, then indicates what is to take place in response to questions from the Jews (John 2:18).

Examine several Nativity hymns from your hymnal or worship resources. (Sing a few, if you wish.) What do they suggest about Jesus' purpose in his incarnate life?

The response Jesus makes in John 2:19-21 clearly relates to what Jesus sees as inevitable—his execution and the resurrection to follow. (A question that has occupied scholars for centuries is whether this early visit by Jesus to Jerusalem in John's Gospel is the same visit described in the Synoptic Gospels as Jesus' final visit to Jerusalem or simply a much earlier visit about which the Synoptic writers either did not know or did not describe in their Gospels.)

Predictions
of the Passion ■

Read Matthew 16:13-20; Mark 8:27-30; and Luke 9:18-21. What is the context for the confession according to each of the Gospel writers? Who is present? Why, do you think, did Jesus order them not to tell anyone that he is the Messiah?

Predictions of the Passion

Throughout the Gospels are predictions made by Jesus of the impending ordeal he must face, predictions of the execution and the subsequent resurrection. These are stated in indirect and on occasion very direct ways. Some of these predictions are couched in conversations with his followers; others Jesus proclaimed to large groups of people, including those who opposed him.

Scholars usually draw attention to three major predictions of the Passion, however, as clear examples of Jesus' awareness of what was to take place in the days ahead. These three predictions appear in the three Synoptic Gospels in very similar ways and very similar words. In the minds of some authorities, these similarities lend great credibility to these statements; these may be among those statements made by Jesus that were so memorable that they are indeed very close to verbatim accounts of what Jesus said.

The first of these predictions took place following the confession on the part of the disciples that Jesus was indeed the Messiah (Matthew 16:13-20; Mark 8:27-30; Luke 9:18-21). Why did this confession take place at this time, about midway through the ministry of Jesus and at a time when the disciples had been with Jesus for a rather extended period of time? Perhaps the disciples had to live with Jesus for some time before they recognized that he was indeed the Messiah. Perhaps they had not been ready prior to that time to make that confession. Perhaps the disciples were not yet sufficiently mature in the faith to realize the inevitability of the execution of Jesus.

Evidently the time had come for Jesus to prepare his inner circle for the difficult consequences of who he was, regardless of whether they immediately understood. So, he predicted that he "must go to Jerusalem and undergo great suffering at the hands of the elders and chief priests and scribes, and be killed, and on the third day be raised" (Matthew 16:21; see also Mark 8:31 and Luke 9:22). Note how direct this prediction is: Jesus tells his followers where these events will take place—the Holy City of Jerusalem—who will be responsible—elders, chief priests, and scribes—and what will happen—he will be killed and on the third day he will be raised.

Here Jesus is not talking in parables or metaphors; he is speaking clearly, directly, overtly. No wonder Peter responds as he does, rebuking Jesus and saying that such will never take place (Matthew 16:22 and Mark 8:32). Peter and the rest are alarmed, and thus begins a subtle conflict between Jesus and the disciples. Jesus is determined to go to Jerusalem to meet his destiny, to fulfill God's plan; and the followers of Jesus seem at times equally determined to keep him from going to Jerusalem, as if staying away from the Holy City might somehow prolong or cancel the inevitable. (See as one of many such examples John 11:8 and the reference back to John 8:59).

The Second Major Prediction

The second of the three major Passion predictions Jesus made was uttered also in

Read Matthew 16:21-22; Mark 8:31-32; and Luke 9:22. What does Jesus predict? How do the disciples react?

Imagine that you were one of the disciples and had just had the confirmation of the most important faith matter of your life: Jesus is the Messiah. How would you feel? What would you be thinking? For news this important, who would be on your mental list to tell?

Next, imagine that Jesus has not only asked, but demanded, that you tell no one. Now how do you feel?

Then the unthinkable happens. Jesus tells you that the pastors, theological school professors, and lay leaders of all the churches are going to treat him horribly and have him killed. Now how do you feel? What would you say or do? How would you deal with your intense feelings? Would you feel any differently about Jesus? about your religious community? Explain.

The Second Prediction ■

Read Matthew 17:22-23; Mark 9:30-32; and Luke

9:43b-45. What, if any-
thing, is different about
this prediction from the
first? Again, assess your
feelings if you had been a
disciple. What would be
going on in your head and
heart now?

How would you define
betrayal? Have you ever
been betrayed by someone
intimately close to you?

In groups of three, take
turns assuming the role of
betrayer, betrayed, and
observer. While we usually
do not act out in extremes,
we may feel like it. Assume
a **pose** that indicates what
you would feel like doing if
you had been betrayed by
an intimate. (This activity
suggests being physical—
but not rough. **Do not insist
that anyone participate
who would prefer not to**

Galilee, far away from Jerusalem. Here again,
the words of Jesus are precise, succinct, clear;
mistaking his meaning and direction is impossible. This second prediction is quoted in
Matthew 17:22-23; Mark 9:30-32; and Luke
9:43b-45. Notice the remarkable similarity of
the wording of these predictions. Again, the
wording is blunt; Matthew and Mark report
Jesus as saying, ". . . they will kill him," referring to himself as the Son of Man. But again,
the man Jesus offers the promise: "on the
third day he will be raised."

Note, however, an addition that Jesus
makes in this prediction, an element not present in the first major prediction of his coming arrest, execution, and resurrection. Jesus
indicates in this second prediction in all
three Synoptic Gospels that he will be
"betrayed." While the Revised Standard
Version uses the word *delivered*, the King
James Version, the New Revised Standard
Version, and the New International Version
use the word *betrayed*.

Consider the impact of this word on the
followers of Jesus. To be betrayed is to be
turned over to evil, to suffering and pain, to
agony by one who has been trusted. To be
betrayed is to be cheated and wronged by
one who has been loved and trusted. Betrayal
is a human act.

Perhaps the followers of Jesus could comprehend evil befalling the innocent or the
faultless; they probably knew well the story
of Job from the Hebrew Scriptures. But
betrayal is an intentional, willful act. It is the
ultimate violation of a trust; it is the epitome
of rejecting love and respect. Betrayal is a
sinful human act that plumbs the depths of
human depravity, for it violates all that is
holy in one's words and one's actions.

Jesus indicated to his followers that he

touch or be touched; this is voluntary. The observer will make sure no one gets *too* involved in the part!)

How did this pose feel in your body? How do you think Jesus might have felt? What might he have wanted to do?

The Third Prediction ■

Read Matthew 20:17-19; Mark 10:32-34; and Luke 18:31-34. What dimension is added to the third prediction? What does the collusion between the Roman leaders and the Jewish religious leaders suggest to you about the inevitability of the Crucifixion? about the desperation of each side: Rome and Israel? about the "strange bedfellows" who unite in a common cause?

would be betrayed. Perhaps it was this word *betrayal* that struck the disciples with such force that "they were greatly distressed" (Matthew 17:23b) and simply "did not understand" what he was saying (Mark 9:32 and Luke 9:45a). That God would visit trials and tribulations on a human being could be comprehended to a point. That a man such as Jesus, who went about doing good for others, preaching and teaching the love of God, would be betrayed was almost inconceivable.

Note how Jesus is building these predictions to a crescendo; each prediction adds another dimension to the description of what is to come. First, Jesus is to be arrested and killed but be raised again on the third day; next this is going to happen because of a betrayal. The third major prediction adds yet another dimension to this scene.

The Third Major Prediction

Jesus' third prediction of his Passion took place as he and the band of followers were making their way toward Jerusalem (Matthew 20:17-19; Mark 10:32-34; and Luke 18:31-34). Again, his words are direct and clear; none can mistake what he is saying for parable or metaphor. Jesus adds more detail to this prediction, as if the disciples would not have been able to handle the horrible details at the first prediction. First, he had told them he would be arrested and crucified; next, that he would be turned over to his enemies by someone he knew and trusted. The third prediction added more detail as to just what would happen in Jerusalem.

In this prediction Jesus places the blame for what is going to happen to him on two groups. The chief priests and scribes (in the passages from Matthew and Mark) make up one group that will prosecute Jesus. The

Bible 301 ☐

In a Bible dictionary, look up scribes, Pharisees, (chief) priest, Gentile. What were their functions? their relationship to each other? to Rome?

It's one thing to be mocked or spit upon; quite another to be flogged. Look up flogging. Think about what it would be like to be beaten in this vicious way, and in Jesus' day, what kind of medical care would be available. (Of course, Jesus didn't get any care; he was going to be killed anyway.) How would the disciples be thinking about suffering now?

What does the fact that Jesus deliberately went toward such pain and ignominy mean to you?

other (reported by Luke) consists of the "Gentiles," that is, the non-Jews; in this case, the Romans. In all three Synoptic Gospels Jesus declares that he will be "handed over" to the Gentiles (in this case, the Romans), by the chief priests and scribes.

Does this mean that the Romans would not have become involved if the chief priests and scribes had not deliberately included them? Probably not. But his statement does suggest that it is the concerted, cooperative action of both groups—chief priests and Roman authorities—that leads to the death of Jesus and to the resurrection to follow. (See, for example, Mark 3:6, where this alliance is formed at the beginning of Jesus' ministry.)

Jesus is not quite finished with this prediction. He goes on to indicate that he will be abused before he is killed. All the Synoptic writers indicate he will be mocked and flogged (Matthew 20:19; Mark 10:34; Luke 18:32-33). Mark and Luke add that he will be spat upon, and Luke further indicates Jesus will be insulted. The three most severe indignities—being mocked, spat upon, and flogged—were punishments reserved for the very dregs of society, for the vilest of the vile.

The Romans delighted in capital punishment, but they allowed some criminals to die with dignity and honor. Not so those who were subjected to the extremes of abuse—the floggings, mockings, and the repulsive experiences of being spat upon. Imagine how the disciples recoiled from this picture. Perhaps they could comprehend their leader dying a warrior's death, but to suffer the ignominy of such abusive and repugnant treatment usually accorded the worst of common criminals was beyond them. Perhaps this is why Luke indicates "they understood nothing about all these things; in fact, what he said was hidden from them, and they did not grasp what was said" (Luke 18:34).

A Unique Prediction

Read at least one of the passages about taking up one's cross: the cost of discipleship. What did it mean for Jesus to take up a cross? How do we use that expression now? (Often it refers to dealing with an inconvenience; not to making a tremendous sacrifice.) Is our current understanding what Jesus really meant, do you think? If not, how should we understand our own "marching orders"?

While Jesus predicted his execution in many other places in the Gospels, one often-repeated statement of his deserves attention. Five times in the Synoptic Gospels Jesus warns his followers that each person must take up his or her cross and follow Jesus in order to be a disciple of Jesus (Matthew 10:38; Matthew 16:24; Mark 8:34; Luke 9:23; and Luke 14:27). While these passages are well known, they contain seeds of very significant predictions of the Passion to come. Consider:

First, the cross was the Roman form of execution; stoning was the Jewish form. No Jewish court would crucify a criminal; to do so was to bring the curse of God upon the whole land (Deuteronomy 21:22-23; see also Paul's analysis of this in Galatians 3:10-14). Therefore, Jesus was indicating clearly by what means he would be killed and at the same time who would ultimately be responsible for his death, that is, the Romans.

Read Deuteronomy 21:22-23. Jesus predicted that he would die by a Roman means of execution and that others of his serious and sincere followers may have to do the same. If you *really* had to take up a cross, would you follow Jesus? What is the greatest threat posed to you for being a follower of Jesus Christ? If you followed even the most radical of Jesus' teachings about discipleship, justice to the poor, and so on, what might be the greatest threat to you? What does this tell you about your own assessment of the cost of discipleship?

Second, Jesus was indicating to his followers that the same dire fate might await them if they chose to follow him (see for example, Mark 10:38-39 and John 21:18-19). What terror such a comment must have struck in the hearts of the disciples! Jesus was in effect telling each of them (to use a modern reference) to bring along an electric chair or a gas chamber or a gallows or a lethal injection gurney if she or he wanted to follow Jesus, for that would surely await the person who chose to follow the wandering preacher from the Galilee.

Third, by this statement Jesus was announcing that his followers had no alternative except total commitment; no such thing as a partial or a halfway commitment to the cause of the Messiah was possible. An individual was either for Jesus or against Jesus; no middle road existed (see, for example, Luke 11:23).

Jesus had made his commitment; he was resolved to complete the mission assigned to him, even though that mission ended at a cross. He warned his disciples that once they had made that same commitment, turning back was impossible ("No one who puts a hand to the plow and looks back is fit for the kingdom of God," Luke 9:62). Those who opposed the man Jesus were growing in power, authority, and perhaps in number. But who were those opposed to him? And why did a man such as Jesus attract opposition dedicated to his destruction?

Closing Prayer ■

Jesus made his commitment and followed it resolutely to the cross. Take time in prayer to consider your own commitment and willingness to "take up the cross." Offer prayer for those whose lives are in danger for the sake of the gospel.

Session Two

Opposition

Session Focus ■

This session focuses on the opposition to Jesus and his ministry by highlighting the major opponents: Rome and the leading Jewish authorities.

Session Objective ■

You will become more thoroughly acquainted with the religious and political structures of Jesus' day and how they worked together to oppose Jesus' ministry.

Session Preparation ■

If possible, obtain a copy of a Gospel parallel, a reference book that lines up together the passages from the Synoptic Gospels that are similar. Your pastor or church library may have a copy.

Choose from among these activities and discussion starters to plan your lesson.

The Political Scene ■

Find a map in the back of your study Bible or in a Bible atlas that shows Palestine and surrounding areas at the time of the rule of Greece and also

To comprehend the opposition to the man Jesus, we must first gain an understanding of the world in which Jesus lived out his ministry. As is the case in our day, Jesus' world consisted of many components; to focus on one or two components is to miss the "big picture" and misunderstand the events leading up to the execution of Jesus. Among the many components of the world of Jesus' time were the political structures and realities of first-century Palestine, the religious world in which Jesus lived, the socioeconomic context of the period, and—always difficult to comprehend in retrospect—the attitude, mindset, or morale of the populace at the time.

The Political Scene: Rome

At the time of the execution of Jesus, Judea was an imperial province of Rome, administered by a Roman procurator or governor appointed by the emperor.

Some history will clarify this point. In 63 B.C., the Roman general Pompey entered Jerusalem after a three-month siege and ended the independence of Judea that had been won by the Maccabeans. It was these Maccabeans, as a group of Jewish patriots were known, who captured Jerusalem from the Syrians in 164 B.C., rededicated the Temple, and in 161 brought some measure of self-rule to Judea. This was the first true independence that nation had known since

during the life of Jesus when Rome ruled the area. How far did those two empires extend? Where is Judea situated, relative to the boundaries of the empire? to the seat of power in Rome or Greece?

Bible 301 □

Skim through the apocryphal books of First and Second Maccabees to get a flavor of the religious writing and understanding of the Jews' conflict with the Greek empire and its Hellenizing practices as well as the hard-won state of affairs in Judea when Rome ended Judea's independence.

Using the map, locate the areas that came under the rule of Philip, Antipas, and Archelaus. Skim through the first two chapters of Matthew and Luke. What Roman rulers are mentioned and what can we learn about them? How do these two Gospel writers set the political tone for what is to come?

the Exile. The apocryphal books of First and Second Maccabees tell the story of this revolt. But this independence was short-lived. Even the zeal of the Maccabeans could not stand up to the internal power struggles among those who followed the Maccabees nor to the power and might of the Roman army when Rome intervened to bring order to the internal political chaos.

Rome was not overly impressed with its conquest. Judea was on the fringe of the Roman Empire; it was not much more than a buffer state containing a rather major north-south trade route. Rome provided little internal administration for Judea for about a generation after the conquest. As a result, Judea was in a state of internal political chaos until Rome finally acted to restore order.

The Roman Empire brought a measure of stability to this chaos by finally appointing a puppet king of Judea, a king who would be directly accountable in all things to Rome. The puppet king appointed by Rome was the infamous Herod. Diabolical, ruthless, insensitive, but nonetheless quite successful, this man was appointed King of Judea in 40 B.C., a throne he held for thirty-six years. Herod more than satisfied his Roman masters, but he was increasingly hated by his subjects. He was not truly Jewish; he was bloodthirsty and vengeful; and he accommodated many foreign cults and practices in Jerusalem.

Upon the death of Herod in 4 B.C., Rome divided his holdings among three of Herod's sons. Philip was placed in charge of the area north and east of the Sea of Galilee. Galilee and the area east of the Jordan River was assigned to Antipas. But the prize, Judea proper, including Jerusalem, as well as Samaria and Idumaea (the area south of Jerusalem) was given to Archelaus.

This last assignment proved to be a major mistake. Archelaus was simply not up to the task of governing the region assigned him. Especially was he unable to govern, that is, control, the Jews of Judea and Jerusalem; for it was here that opposition to Rome was most intense and focused. Rome tolerated the ineffectiveness and bungling of Archelaus for about ten years, then removed him from all offices and exiled him. After A.D. 6, Archelaus apparently drops from history's records.

Rome was still faced with "what to do" with Judea. Judea was still too insignificant to merit rule by a Roman *legate* or high-ranking Roman bureaucrat such as ruled most imperial provinces. Instead, Judea was ruled by a Roman governor or *procurator*. After a string of other rulers, Pontius Pilate was assigned to Judea. He held his office from A.D. 26 to 36.

Pilate had considerable power, although he and many other of his predecessors could and often did rely heavily on the Judean structures and institutions already in place to control the populace and allowed the Judean courts a great deal of leeway in administering the internal laws of the land.

The Sanhedrin

The Sanhedrin

After reading this description of the Sanhedrin, what is your understanding of how it worked and who was on it?

The principal Judean court, and the court on which the Roman governors or procurators relied heavily, was the Sanhedrin, a council of the local elite along with some Roman oversight. The president of the Sanhedrin was the high priest, although the designation "high priest" was also given to former holders of that office and to the male relatives of the current high priest. Thus, the term "chief priests" was often used to emphasize the priests on

Bible 301 □

*Using a Bible dictionary,
look up* Sanhedrin *and*
council, *and, if you haven't
done so already,* (chief)
priest, scribe, *and* elder.
*What more complete pic-
ture do you get of the
membership, organization,
and purpose of this ruling
council?*

the Sanhedrin as differentiated from the
high priest or president of the body—at the
time of Jesus a man named Caiaphas. The
lay members of the Sanhedrin were
referred to as "elders," "scribes," and
Pharisees, though these designations were
not mutually exclusive.

Thus, when the biblical text refers, as it
so often does, to "chief priests, scribes, and
elders" (see, for example, Mark 11:27;
14:43; and Luke 9:22) the text is referring
to members of the Sanhedrin or to the
Sanhedrin as a gathered body. The
Sanhedrin ruled at the pleasure of the governor, and the governor or procurator
relied heavily on the Sanhedrin to maintain
order and peace in Judea. The local rulers
were judged in part on their ability to
maintain order (and collect taxes) in the
province, and in many ways the Sanhedrin
became an arm of this maintenance of
order and control.

Rome
and Sanhedrin ■

Form several small groups
or work individually. Divide
all or most of the Scripture
references in this section
among the small groups.
What does the passage say
about the power structure
of the day and about that
structure's understanding
of Jesus and his ministry?
Why would his activity be
irritating, alarming, or
threatening?

Rome and Sanhedrin Oppose Jesus

Clearly, the Gospels indicate over and
over again that many of the members of the
Sanhedrin were opposed to the man Jesus.
The reasons for this opposition are obvious. Jesus was fomenting dissatisfaction
with the prevailing political structures of
Judea. Jesus was speaking of a spiritual
kingdom at a time when his followers were
looking for an earthly king. He was an itinerant preacher who gathered large crowds;
and to the eyes of the procurators and the
Sanhedrin, any large crowd of common
people was dangerous. Such a crowd could
become an uncontrollable mob very quickly, threatening the control and order that
Rome dictated (see for example Matthew
27:15-24).

Assume the role of a particular leader according to the passage you read. (For example, Matthew 5:41 aligns you with Rome; Luke 19:45-46, with the Jewish religious leaders.) Gather in the two different identity groups, review your Scripture, and discuss why this Jesus means trouble to you. Given the power at your disposal, what do you think you should do about him?

Perhaps another reason why some in the political forces were opposed to Jesus was their difficulty in comprehending his message. On the one hand, Jesus counseled cooperating with the Roman authorities (Matthew 5:41 refers to the right of a Roman soldier to require a Judean to carry his gear for a mile; see also Matthew 22:15-21; Mark 12:13-17; and Luke 20:20-26); but on the other hand (and in some of these very same passages) Jesus demanded primary allegiance to God rather than to Rome or even to the Sanhedrin. While Jesus indicated that no one can serve two masters, God and wealth (Matthew 6:24; Luke 16:13), he was certainly also implying that the people could not serve both God and Rome. To those in control, these were seditious words.

Jesus' actions threatened the peace and order of the time. His miracles upset the natural order of events; his preaching led people away from allegiance to Rome and toward full allegiance to God; and his righteous indignation in cleansing the Temple (John 2:13-17; Matthew 21:10-13; Mark 11:15-17; Luke 19:45-46) stimulated some of the members of the Sanhedrin to renew their efforts to find a way to have Jesus executed (Mark 11:18; Luke 19:47).

Even Jesus' entry into Jerusalem on what we know as Palm Sunday could be viewed as mocking the Roman conquerors (Matthew 21:1-9; Mark 11:1-10; Luke 19:28-38). Jesus probably came in through the same Eastern Gate that victorious Roman generals entered. But Jesus came astride a lowly beast of burden, a donkey, rather than on a prancing white stallion, as was the custom of the Roman military victors. Also, Jesus came into Jerusalem to the welcoming cheers of the rabble of the city, not the shouts of the upper classes of the populace. Did Jesus intend his Palm Sunday actions as a mockery of Rome? Perhaps not, but those actions probably had that effect on the occupying forces.

Religious Structures ■

Try to identify with the Jews' "seamless" intersection of religion and politics. Judea was supposed to be a theocracy; a nation ruled by God through the temporal leaders. Is there any sort of contemporary parallel or comparison? If the US were truly a Christian nation, for example, and our constitution had to adhere only to biblical principles, how might our governance and politics be different?

The Religious Structures at the Time of Jesus

Twenty-first–century citizens of the United States of America have difficulty comprehending the close intertwining of religion with politics in ancient Judea. Our contemporary insistence on the separation of church and state gives us no experience in understanding how institutionalized religion and political structures can overlap, intermix, and be mutually dependent on one another. We must try to enter the world of first-century Judea to grasp this concept fully.

At the outset, suffice it to say that the Roman authorities had little interest in the religious practices of first-century Judeans. If religion could help hold the people in check and under control, fine; if religion threatened the dominance of Rome (as Christianity did in the second century), then that religion must be stamped out. Thus, the governors or procurators generally had a "live-and-let-live" attitude toward the religious practices of the Jews as long as those religious practices did not threaten the order imposed by Rome.

For the Judeans themselves, however, religion and politics, religious institutions and government institutions were inextricably mixed. Religious parties were political; political parties were religious; no separation between church and state existed.

The various religious-political parties in Judea are well-known; suffice it here to provide a very quick review:

The Zealots

Who were the Zealots? What was their understanding of the theocratic identity of the Jews?

If the Romans had reason to fear any of the major religious-political parties, they had reason to fear the Zealots. Put most simply, the Zealots were theocrats; they believed that only God had the right to rule the Jews. Thus, the Zealots were ultra-patriots, fanatically committed to their Jewish faith and to their devotion to the law of Moses. Because of these beliefs, they were revolutionaries, but not a well-organized resistance movement as we would think of one today.

The Zealots were committed to using every means possible to drive the Romans from Judea and to return Judea to a theocracy; that is, a land in which God alone was king. The Zealots counseled noncooperation with everything Roman and constantly engaged in a variety of acts of terrorism against the Roman rule. From about the mid-first century, after the Crucifixion, members of an extreme wing of the Zealots were known for, among many other acts of terrorism, secreting long slender daggers (*sicarii*) in their robes in order to murder Roman soldiers and officials in crowded marketplaces. They were thus also known as the *Sicarii*, or Assassins.

Read Luke 6:15 and Acts 1:13-14. Why, do you think, would Jesus invite a Zealot to be part of his inner circle? Why, do you think, would he have had only one, and not all twelve?

The origin of the Zealots is uncertain, though they traced some of their beliefs and practices back to the Maccabees. The Jewish historian Josephus traces the Zealots to at least A.D. 6 and a revolt against Roman taxes led by a man named Judas of Galilee (see Acts 5:37).

Though it is unlikely, suppose Judas Iscariot was a Zealot. Would this make any difference in our understanding of his actions? If he were an assassin, or at least willing to kill to achieve his goals, why, do you think, would he have arranged for Jesus'

At least one of the twelve disciples was a Zealot, for Luke 6:15 and Acts 1:13 name Simon the Zealot. A few scholars have suggested that Judas Iscariot may have been a Zealot, indeed a member of the *Sicarii*, for the name "Iscariot" may mean *Sicarii*. But

death, and not for one or more of the Jewish or Roman rulers?

Opposition by Zealots ■

Jesus was "zealous" for God. Why, do you think, would his actions have carried little appeal for the Zealots?

more authorities suggest that the name "Iscariot" merely indicates that Judas was from the village of Kerioth.

Opposition to Jesus by the Zealots

Why, then, would Zealots be opposed to Jesus? Several reasons are possible:

Although Jesus did engage in some revolutionary acts and revolutionary rhetoric, for the Zealots he was not acting quickly nor decisively enough. His words of cooperation with the Romans (such as agreeing to pay taxes) were repugnant to the Zealots. The man Jesus made grandiose claims about new kings and new kingdoms, but he did not demonstrate either the will or the ability to create a militarily successful revolutionary army that would accomplish the Zealot goal of ridding Judea of the Romans. Bear in mind that, for the Zealots, military victory over the Romans was the only kind of victory that mattered; their ears were deaf to Jesus' preaching of the kingdom of God in other forms.

The Zealots were perhaps not so much opposed to Jesus as they were disappointed and disgusted with him. Here was another potentially promising charismatic leader who had the skill to marshal people to his side but who seemed to lack the will or the desire to construct of those people a military force that could lead a revolution. To the Zealots, Jesus was a suddenly rising star who in their opinion just as quickly burned out. His goals were clearly not their goals.

Sadduceean Opposition ■

Summarize this religious and political profile of the Sadducees. Use a concordance to see how often the

Sadduceean Opposition

The aristocracy of Judea was opposed to anything and anyone who threatened its place, position, and prestige—to saying nothing of its wealth!—and Jesus threatened the aristocracy.

Sadducees appear in the Scriptures and look up several of the references. (See Matthew 3; 16; 22; Acts 4; 5; 23.) What portrait emerges? Who, in our religious institutions, might correspond to the office or role held by the Sadducees? (Are they "bad guys"?) How might defenders of the faith be misunderstood, especially if their stand is a lonesome one, or, on the other hand, if they lose sight of what is essential?

Bible 301 ☐

Look up Greece, Greek, or Hellenization in a Bible dictionary in order to understand the process and ideals of Hellenization. Why, if it was antithetical to the Jewish religion, would the Sadducees embrace it? What were the benefits? What was the cost of maintaining or supporting the policies and ideology of Greece that Rome continued?

Much of the aristocracy of Judea were Sadducees. These people were (or considered themselves to be) descendants of the high priestly line descended from Zadok, the high priest at the time of King David and a descendant of Aaron. The Sadducees held inherited wealth; and through their activities in the Sanhedrin they wielded great political power.

The Sadducees were well represented in the Sanhedrin, for they were the priestly caste. It was Sadducees who were in charge of the Temple and the sacrifices and services that were conducted there. It was from the Sadducees that the high priest was selected (at the time of Jesus, by Rome!), and it was to the Sadducees that most of the "chief priests" belonged.

The Sadducees were conservative in matters of religion. They held to only the first five books of the Law (while other groups, including Jesus) believed in other books in what has become the Hebrew canon. They held to the laws of Moses in the Torah, but refused to accept any revelation of God after Moses. They practiced and taught a literal interpretation of the Law; and they rejected theological concepts that arose in "later" Jewish religion, such as the resurrection of the dead, eternal life, and angels and demons.

The Sadducees were liberal politically. They counseled extreme cooperation with Rome (as a way of securing their own status) and they favored the Hellenization of Judea. "Hellenization" refers to the spreading of Greek influence, culture, values, and so on. Devout non-Sadducean Jews, especially the Pharisees, were aghast at this notion, for Hellinization is precisely what had stimulated the Maccabean Revolt of 168 B.C. (see, as one example, 2 Maccabees 4:7-17).

In some ways, the attitude of the

Sadducees was an attitude of trying to save Judea. They knew of the destruction of the land that preceded the Exile; they knew of Pompey's destruction of Jerusalem. They were intent on doing whatever was necessary to preserve their land and their way of life. And if this preservation of all in which they believed demanded some accommodation with Rome, some "watering down" of principles, so be it. They would remain wealthy, they would continue to enjoy their status as the aristocracy, and they would continue in power.

Put most succinctly, the Sadducees were bitterly opposed to anything or anyone who threatened the status quo, and that is precisely what Jesus did. Jesus taught the *interpretation* of the law rather than the *letter* of the law. He taught from books other than the five books of Moses. He had the audacity to question Temple practices that had long been part of the tradition of the Sadducees, and he declared himself time and again Son of God and Son of Man, titles to which no human being ought to assume, according to the Sadducees.

Armed with the authority of the Sanhedrin and with their priestly powers, many of the Sadducees could be and were actively opposed to Jesus. For some of the Sadducees, the opposition was religious; for others, the opposition stemmed from what they perceived as a threat to their power, prestige, and wealth. What threatened Rome threatened them, although that attitude put the Sadducees at odds with much of the rest of Judean society.

The Pharisees

A large religious group in Judea at the time of Jesus—and a group frequently mis-

In small groups, brainstorm a list of four or five important cultural, political, or religious shifts that occurred in the last half of the twentieth century. Imagine that one of your main goals prior to the shift was to maintain the status quo—and you have some power or authority to do it.

What was the "status quo" at the time? What was being challenged? How might our lives be different if the shift had never taken place? Is there really any way to stop these shifts from occurring? In what way might we defend the actions of the Sadducees? question them?

The Pharisees ■

Summarize this religious Pharisees. Use a concordance to see how often the Pharisees appear in the Scriptures, and look up several of the references. (There will be considerably more than for the Sadducees!)

What portrait emerges? What were their values and principles? What position, in our religious institutions, might correspond to the office or role held by the Pharisees? (Are they "bad guys"?) How might the Pharisees have been misunderstood, especially if their observance of the law was pleasing to God? How might they have lost their way?

understood—was the Pharisees. The Pharisees shared several common characteristics:

- The Pharisees were laypersons; they were not priests.
- The Pharisees were clearly what we would deem middle-class; most were merchants and tradespeople.
- The Pharisees were strictly monotheistic; but they were more liberal than the Sadducees in terms of the authority for that monotheism. As mentioned above, they, unlike the Sadducees, held to the Torah, the Prophets, the Writings (Psalms, Proverbs, and other books), and the oral tradition as authoritative in matters of faith.
- The Pharisees focused on the study of the law; they considered the study of the law to be true worship. In this, the Pharisees were responsible for shifting Judaism from a religion of sacrifice to a religion of law, a characteristic that continues to this day.
- The Pharisees concentrated on religious acts such as sabbath keeping, tithing, and ritual purification. Their emphasis on purification caused them to separate themselves from those ritually unclean, and thus the Pharisees became a sect that practiced exclusivity. This exclusive attitude made the Pharisees appear (and in many cases be) self-centered, self-righteous, and self-sufficient.
- The Pharisees generally held in contempt the 'Am Ha'arez, the people of the land, what we would call the peasants. Nevertheless, the people had a high regard for the scribes, some of whom were Pharisees.
- The Pharisees made use of established synagogues as centers for the study of the law;

Now imagine one or more of those cultural, political, religious shifts and imagine what it would be like to have to maintain a strict interpretation of the law or the rules. If the rules had not bent or broken during that shift, what might life be like now?

Opposition by Pharisees ■

Look up two or three of the stories about Jesus healing on the sabbath. What was the objection of the Pharisees? If God commanded rest on one day, is it up to humans to decide when some other activity takes priority? If they were protecting the sabbath and trying to ensure that worship, an attendance upon God, were the focus, how could what they espoused have been wrong or set aside? In our day, when nearly every retail business is open on Sunday, is there a lesson to learn from the Pharisees?

Look up these passages about doing work on the sabbath. What does it mean that the sabbath was made for humankind, not the other way around? When does one cross the

they exercised effective control over the synagogues and over the teachings that took place in there.

• Because of their status, and because of their authority in the synagogues, the Pharisees exercised considerable influence over the general population.

Opposition to Jesus by the Pharisees

Of the groups within first-century Judea with which Jesus had differences, perhaps the Pharisees are best known. The Gospels are filled with accounts of his conflicts with Pharisees. This has led a few scholars to suggest that Jesus himself may have been a Pharisee and that he was more critical of the group of which he was a part than he may have been of groups with which he was not involved. If Joseph, the earthly father of Jesus, were a carpenter, he may have been of the middle-class and quite possibly a Pharisee. But the opposition of the Pharisees to Jesus took a number of different forms:

Jesus rejected the strict observance of the sabbath, a particularly egregious fault in the eyes of the Pharisees. For example, Jesus healed on the sabbath (Matthew 12:9-14; Mark 3:1-6; Luke 6:6-11; 13:10-17; 14:1-6; John 5:1-16; 9:1-41) even though curing an illness was considered work. "There are six days on which work ought to be done; come on those days and be cured, and not on the sabbath day" (Luke 13:14b) was the complaint of the Pharisees. Healing was not appropriate for the sabbath.

Jesus compounded his apparent rejection of sabbath keeping by allowing his followers to undertake the work of plucking and preparing grain for eating on a sabbath (Matthew 12:1-8; Mark 2:23-28; Luke 6:1-5). To emphasize his view of the sabbath, so at

line from obedience to God's will to neglecting the weightier matters of the law: justice, mercy, and faith? How do you know? How do you guard against it?

odds with the perspective of the Pharisees, Jesus declared that "the sabbath was made for humankind, and not humankind for the sabbath" (Mark 2:27).

Jesus challenged the understandings of the Pharisees about tithing, arguing that they put far too much emphasis on the act and failed to grasp its meaning (Matthew 23:23). Jesus was not criticizing the practice of tithing necessarily; but he was arguing with the minute attention to the details of the law that would require a Pharisee to tithe one-tenth of the dill weed or one-tenth of the mint leaves the Pharisee had collected to season his food, while at the same time neglecting "the weightier matters of the law: justice, mercy, and faith. It is these you ought to have practiced without neglecting the others" (Matthew 23:23). Jesus was telling the Pharisees, experts in the law, that they misunderstood and misused the law!

What does it mean now to lead a life that is pure? What makes one pure? What liturgical rituals or practices do we have that are concerned with purity?

Jesus challenged the understandings of the Pharisees about purification. By the first century, the Pharisee's daily life was encompassed with purification ritual after purification ritual. Ritual handwashing, ritual dishwashing, and ritual cleansing occupied much of the Pharisee's time and effort. Again, Jesus proclaimed to the Pharisees that they were missing the entire point of purification. In

Read Matthew 15:11 and surrounding verses to get the context. How does this passage speak to inner purity? Why would it have been galling to the Pharisees?

scathing terms of denunciation (including some name-calling!), Jesus proclaims, "For you clean the outside of the cup and of the plate, but inside they are full of greed and self-indulgence. You blind Pharisee! First clean the inside of the cup, so that the outside also may become clean" (Matthew 23:25b-26). So too with the Pharisaic attention to clean and unclean food; Jesus explained that "it is not what goes into the mouth that defiles a person, but it is what comes out of the mouth that defiles" (Matthew 15:11; see also Mark 7:15).

Again and again, Jesus demonstrated to those who prided themselves on their mastery of the law that they simply did not comprehend the law or its purpose and that their very devotion to the law was leading to their destruction because of their misunderstanding.

But perhaps one of the most galling (to the Pharisees) of the actions of the man Jesus was his forgiveness of sins. Reread the story of the paralytic carried to Jesus by four friends, the story of letting the lame man down before Jesus through a hole in the roof (Matthew 9-1-8; Mark 2:1-12; Luke 5:17-26). The first response of Jesus to this action on the part of the four men and the paralytic was not to heal the paralytic but to forgive his sins. Immediately, according to Luke, the scribes and Pharisees challenged this, saying that only God can forgive sins.

Either Jesus was proclaiming a patent lie, or, far worse, Jesus was equating himself with God. For the Pharisees, this was inconceivable on the one hand and the height of apostasy on the other. They simply could not tolerate in their midst one who would claim such power for himself. Jesus compounded this audacity when, in the very home of a Pharisee, he forgave the sins of a woman who was known to be a sinner (Luke 7:36-50). Again, the question: "Who is this who even forgives sins?" (Luke 7:49).

As a final example of the actions of Jesus that caused the bitter opposition of many of the Pharisees, the Synoptic writers record Jesus listing for his disciples and for the crowds the sins of the Pharisees (Matthew 23:1-36, with parallels in Mark and Luke). Hear again the litany of their shortcomings:

Read the story of the paralyzed man from one of the Gospels. Have a few volunteers pantomime the story while someone reads it aloud. Have other group members be Pharisees and others in the crowd gathered to hear Jesus.

Imagine that you (if you're part of the crowd) are sitting inside while mud and dust fall into your hair and lap while the ones on the roof dig through. Think through just how that scene must have been played out, and then hear Jesus say the ill man's sins are forgiven. Can he do that? Who does he think he is? What do you make of this radical announcement? of Jesus for having said it?

Examine the Scriptures that mention the Pharisees' shortcomings. If you were a seminary professor or a professor of religion at a nearby college or university, how would you feel about having those charges hurled at you? If Jesus—someone you knew as an itinerant preacher—had impugned your values to that extent, what would you think of it? What would you do?

Summarize the main players in the unfolding Passion drama and review the objections of each group. (In retrospect, it seems hard for anyone not to have seen it coming!)

Closing Prayer ■

Gather your thoughts around the ways in which you oppose the gospel. Take some time in reflection or prayer to make or renew your commitment to Jesus Christ. Offer prayer that we may overcome the forces that oppose God's will.

hypocrisy (Matthew 23:2-3); conceit and self-righteousness (23:5-7); self-exaltation (23:12); false teaching of many kinds, based on basic misunderstandings of God's will (23:13-22); and the aforementioned mistaken emphasis on tithing and purification (23:23-26). And Jesus spares no punches; he refers to the Pharisees as "whitewashed tombs" (23:27), beautiful to behold on the outside but lifeless, impure, and filthy within. He climaxes his denunciation of the party of the Pharisees by unabashedly calling them, "You snakes, you brood of vipers!" and challenging them with "How can you escape being sentenced to hell?" (23:33).

Can any doubt about the Pharisees' opposition to Jesus remain? He had challenged them at the very core of their being and impugned the values they held most sacred. This was no ordinary wandering preacher; this man had to be stopped.

Session Three

Sunday Through Thursday

Session Focus

This session focuses on the events of what we call Holy Week and how the opposition to Jesus came to a head after the Passover meal.

Session Objective

You will become better acquainted with some of particular pilgrim practices followed by Jesus and his disciples and the meaning of those practices.

Session Preparation

Have on hand the Gospel parallel, a Bible atlas, and several copies of your denomination's hymnal.

Choose from among these activities and discussion starters to plan your lesson.

On the Way to Jerusalem ■

Use the Bible atlas or a map of Palestine in your study Bible to locate the probable route Jesus and his disciples took from Galilee to Jerusalem by way of the eastern bank of the Jordan River. If travelers on foot could cover

The die had been cast; all was in readiness. Jesus gathered his followers and made his way to Jerusalem for the Passover. The opposition to him had formed and hardened; all the groups that found reason to want Jesus silenced were in place. That Jesus knew what would take place on his final trip to Jerusalem was unquestionable. He had talked with his disciples about this situation time and again. They counseled him not to go, but he was determined. He would be in Jerusalem for the Passover; and while there, those forces arrayed against him would work their will.

On the Way to Jerusalem

So Jesus left Galilee for the last time before his execution. He made his way toward Jerusalem, probably entering Judea from the east side of the Jordan River (Matthew 19:1 and Mark 10:1). While Matthew suggests that part of Judea lay beyond (that is, east of) the Jordan River, Mark's account may be more accurate. In Mark, Jesus crossed the Jordan, traveled south, down the eastern side of the river, then crossed back into Judea at the northern boundary of the Dead Sea. This was not an unusual route for it avoided Samaria, which many pious Jews did. Jesus refused to do so on several other occasions (for example, John 4:1-5 and Luke 17:11).

about fifteen miles a day, about how long might it have taken Jesus to arrive?

Choose one or more of the "on the way to Jerusalem" events recorded in the three Synoptic Gospels and look them up. (You may find the Gospel parallel and the atlas useful here.) What happened? Does the Bible tell where it happened? (If so, locate the place on the map.) Who was present? Who was helped, and who, if anyone, was angered or alienated by Jesus' actions or words? What does the incident tell you about Jesus and about his journey to Jerusalem?

You may choose also (or instead) to study one of the events recorded by only one or two of the Gospels. If the event is not recorded in all, why might that be? Is there special significance to that Gospel writer, based on what you know of his purpose and audience? How does the event contribute to the over-arching story of Jesus' trip to Jerusalem?

The Synoptic Gospels agree on several significant events on the way to Jerusalem, such as

- the blessing of the children (Matthew 19:13-15; Mark 10:13-16; Luke 18:15-17);
- the encounter with the rich young man (Matthew 19:16-30; Mark 10:17-31; Luke 18:18-30);
- the third Passion prediction (Matthew 20:17-19; Mark 10:32-34; Luke 8:31-34);
- the request of the sons of Zebedee (Matthew 20:20-28; Mark 10:35-45; see also Luke 22:24-27); and
- the healing of the blind (Matthew 20:29-34; Mark 10:46-52; Luke 18:35-43).

A reading of these accounts is informative; it demonstrates the close similarity between Matthew and Mark's Gospels and displays Luke's Gospel as dealing with similar subjects but in slightly different ways.

Significant also are the stories that are inserted into the account by one or another of the Gospel writers, such as the story of the laborers in the vineyard (Matthew 20:1-16) and Luke's account of Zacchaeus (Luke 19:1-10). (Note that the stories of the healing of Bartimaeus and the story of Zacchaeus are placed in or near Jericho. Jericho is northeast of Jerusalem, suggesting again that Jesus entered Judea from the east.)

Finally the group arrived at Bethphage and Bethany, villages on the eastern slope of the Mount of Olives and on the road between Jericho and Jerusalem (Matthew 21:1; Mark 11:1; and Luke 19:29). Jerusalem was just over the crest of the Mount of Olives and across the Kidron Valley. Quite possibly, the walls of Jerusalem may have been visible from vantage points around these villages. According to Mark, it was the first day of the week, Sunday by our calendar.

A Holy Week Chronology

Matthew and Mark have an almost identical order of events, but do not place all of them on the same days. Mark's first day was what we would identify as Sunday; Matthew's was Monday. They "catch up to each other" with the discovery of the withered fig tree on Tuesday; but for Matthew, it is day two and for Mark it is day three. If we reckon the events by day one, day two, and so on, Mark, for the most part, is a day ahead. If we identify the event by Tuesday, Wednesday, and so on, they are generally together.

Jerusalem at Passover

Read Numbers 9:1-14 and Numbers 19 for the purification laws and rituals. What would anyone have to do in order to participate in the Passover meal? How long would these rites take and who would have to participate? Why would Jesus, the Son of God, have to participate in a purification rite?

We don't follow these laws (or observe the Passover) but we do participate in sacraments and sacramental events. Do you think some sort of preparatory ritual would be necessary? useful? edifying? purifying? If so, what might that preparation include and why? Where should it be done and by whom?

Jerusalem at Passover

Matthew and Mark suggest that Jesus and his followers stayed in Bethany (Matthew 21:17; Mark 11:11); Luke suggests that Jesus and those about him spent the nights of this fateful week on the Mount of Olives (Luke 21:37). Many pilgrims to the city of Jerusalem camped on the hillsides or in the valleys that surrounded the city.

Almost all pilgrims to the city, including Jesus and his followers, arrived several days in advance of the Passover, a very common custom. Passover could not be observed by anyone "unclean," necessitating the appropriate ritual purification rites. The Law forbade anyone who had had recent contact with a corpse from participating in the Passover on the fourteenth day of the first month, the high holy day. Such persons had to wait a month and celebrate what has been called a "supplementary Passover" (Numbers 9:1-14).

Thanks in part to the oral law of the Pharisees, the definition of "contact with a corpse" was very broad. Being in a room with a corpse, touching a corpse, or even walking over a grave could render a person ritually unclean to participate in the Passover. Numbers 19 also records the purification ritual. This process, lasting at least a week, involved being sprinkled twice with a mixture of water and the ashes of a red heifer and participating in several purifying baths. These rituals required the participation of a priest, which means they were to be done at a "sanctuary"; in this case, the Temple.

Jesus and his followers, along with hundreds or perhaps thousands of others, may have arrived in Jerusalem early in order to be purified for the Passover. This may explain his Sunday arrival leading up to the meal on the First Day of the Unleavened Bread "when the Passover lamb is sacrificed" (Mark 14:12; with parallels in Matthew 26:17 and Luke 22:7) on Thursday.

Entering Jerusalem ■

Read each of the accounts of Jesus' entry into Jerusalem (using the Gospel parallel). How are the reports similar? different? Do those differences actually make any difference? If so, what?

Bible 301 ☐

Look at the Palm Sunday hymns in your denominational hymnal. How do they preserve the entry into Jerusalem? Do they add anything that is not actually in the Bible? How do they help you get a flavor of what the event must have been like?

Entering Jerusalem

Jesus' entry into Jerusalem is well-documented (Matthew 21:1-9; Mark 11:1-10; Luke 19:28-38; and John 12:12-19). Tradition reports that he entered through the eastern or Golden Gate, the gate always used by triumphal processions of dignitaries or military heroes. In many ways, Jesus emulated these processions, but in a reverse way.

He chose the humblest of beasts, a donkey, as his mode of transportation. How Jesus obtained the donkey is a matter of conjecture. The three Synoptic Gospels report a wonderful story about Jesus' foreknowledge of man willing to give the disciples a donkey for this purpose; John omits this story altogether.

The significance of the event centered around Jesus' means of transportation and who welcomed him as he entered the Holy City. Jesus was greeted with warmth and excitement by the "rabble" and with growing antagonism by the chief priests, scribes, and Pharisees (for example, Luke 19:39-44 and John 12:19).

In the Temple ■

Read the four Gospel accounts about Jesus in the Temple. If your study Bible has a diagram of the Temple, locate the Court of Gentiles.

Imagine the setting: a huge barn and slaughterhouse; "cowboys" (or the equivalent) who cared for the animals; merchants and bankers who engaged in commerce with thousands of people; enough priests and Levites to do the ritual butchering of sacrificial animals; Temple police keeping order with thousands of strangers in town; and Jesus' little band of Twelve (plus onlookers) in the midst of all those other people. How does the account in the Bible (lacking in detail) color the picture of what happened when Jesus "cleansed" the Temple? Does it make any difference to your understanding of the event or of Jesus' action to realize that he was just one person in the midst of thousands and a huge operation? How do you interpret Jesus' rage? John's addition that Jesus carried a weapon of sorts?

In the Temple

As did almost all of the Jewish pilgrims to Jerusalem, Jesus and his followers immediately made their way to the Temple (Matthew 21:12; Mark 11:11; and Luke 19:45). Like all laypersons, Jesus could enter the courts of the Temple precinct, but not the Temple proper, the sanctuary with its holy place. This encounter took place in the Court of Gentiles, which anyone could enter. What Jesus found enraged him.

The Temple precinct was large and secured by the Temple police—with help from Roman soldiers during the major festivals. Included there was a money exchange and huge kind of barn with stalls for thousands of animals for sacrifice, a place for the animal caretakers to stay, and a slaughterhouse—all necessitated by the requirement of unblemished animals for sacrifice and the specific Tyrian coinage acceptable in the Temple.

While these services were necessary and valuable, they were subject to abuse. Jesus' complaint about "making it [the Temple] a den of robbers" (Matthew 21:13; Mark 11:17; Luke 19:45-46; John 2:16) may have referred to the potential for corruption or to the use of the Temple as a haven for those who had sinned elsewhere.

Jesus exhibited his rage by opening the stalls and cages and turning over the tables of the money changers. John adds that Jesus used a whip made of cords (a weapon of sorts!). Jesus and his little band could only have disrupted the business of this enormous enterprise momentarily, Nevertheless, his point was made in the same memorable style as the prophets who delivered their message with symbolic actions and unusual props (see, for example Ezekiel 4:1-8).

Several dimensions of this story stand out. The first is Jesus' zealous passion for the Temple and for the proper worship of God. Second is Jesus' rage; a man with the passion of Jesus must also be armed with a temper that is held under control until needed. Third is the reaction of those in the Temple area; imagine the picture of animals running around untethered, birds flapping their wings, coins rolling across the pavement with people chasing them, men shouting and cursing, and the followers of Jesus perhaps cowering in amazement. None of the Gospels report the presence of Roman soldiers, but in all probability soldiers put in an appearance to quell the disturbance.

What the Scriptures call the "cleansing" of the Temple implies a more far-reaching result than Jesus no doubt achieved. Nevertheless, this disruption surely was one more event that solidified opposition to the itinerant carpenter-preacher from the Galilee.

What sort of "cleansing" might have taken place, and what was the significance of it? If you were to "cleanse the Temple"—our religious institutions or churches—what "Temple" would you choose, and what would you do?

The Days in Jerusalem ■

Choose one or more of the random teachings from these portions of the Synoptic Gospels. They suggest that although Jesus had an ultimate purpose in Jerusalem that there was also time for "business as usual"—feeding the hungry flock on the

The Days in Jerusalem

After Jesus' disturbance in the Temple, he appears to have gone back each day during that last fateful week to teach (Matthew 21:23–25:46; Mark 11:27–13:37; and Luke 20:1–21:38). Some scholars suggest that some of these teachings might have taken place at other times and other places and that the Gospel writers placed them in this position, not knowing exactly where these

word of God. What was Jesus teaching? Might these hearers have been among those who later cried, "Crucify him!"? If you were soon to reach your last lesson in faith to teach or to hear, what would you want it to be? Why?

The First Day ■

Read the Passover preparation accounts in Matthew 26:17-19; Mark 14:12-16; and Luke 22:7-13. How is the Passover meal to be prepared and observed?

teachings belonged. The somewhat random assortment of teachings and stories and the lack of consistency among the Synoptic Gospels would lend credence to this position.

But whatever transpired during that final week, the opposition to Jesus was growing in intensity and resolve. The Synoptic Gospels tell the story: "They conspired to arrest Jesus by stealth and kill him" (Matthew 26:4; Mark 14:1; Luke 22:2). The end was near; Jesus knew it, and he prepared his followers for it.

The First Day of Unleavened Bread

We actually know little about the specific Passover observance before about A.D. 200. By Matthew's chronology, it was what we call Thursday, the first day of Unleavened Bread. He tells us on this day the Passover Lamb was to be slaughtered and sacrificed (Matthew 26:17; Mark 14:12; Luke 22:7). (Mark conflates the day of preparation and the first day when the meal was eaten.) Each family was to take an unblemished lamb to the Temple to be slaughtered and ritually and symbolically sacrificed, then returned to the family. The family would roast the lamb, then consume it the next day as a family on the first day of Unleavened Bread with ritual prayers and blessings.

Jesus and his band may have followed this pattern in preparation for celebrating the first day of Unleavened Bread. Notice that the disciples of Jesus were very concerned that the rituals for this special meal be followed closely. They asked Jesus where they should make preparations for the Passover meal, and, much like he had done in obtaining the donkey for his Palm Sunday ride, Jesus sent them into the city to find a partic-

Bible 301 ☐

Look up Passover *in a Bible dictionary. What further details shed light on Jesus' observance of this important meal? Read Exodus 12:1-27 to learn more about the original institution of the ritual and the Passover event that it commemorates.*

Gathering for the Meal ■

Read Luke 7:36-50 to get a mental image of what meal time was like for a festive occasion.

ular man who would show them where to prepare for the Passover (Matthew 26:17-19; Mark 14:12-16; Luke 22:7-13).

The Passover was a family meal to be eaten in the home of the family (even if this "home" were a temporary tent within the city walls of Jerusalem, the only legitimate place to observe Passover). But Jesus has the Passover meal with his followers. By so doing, Jesus is declaring that these followers, even the one who betrayed him and those who had so misunderstood him, are his family. The followers of Jesus were saying the same things by their act of sharing this meal with Jesus. Each of them in his own way was saying that Jesus was his family, that his allegiance to Jesus surpassed allegiance even to his own family.

Gathering for the Meal

Most likely, the Supper began at sundown, the first day of Unleavened Bread. Almost certainly, those who gathered for the meal reclined on a couch around a low circular table. Each guest lay on his left side, diagonally on the couch with his feet extending off the back and cradling his head in his left hand. He used his right hand to reach onto the table and into the common bowls of food. As many as three guests might share the same couch.

Looking down from the ceiling on such a meal, the guests resembled the spokes of a wheel, the hub of a wheel being the table in the center. This is why the Gospels tell of the apostle leaning on Jesus' breast. Imagine simply leaning backward as you are reclining on your left side onto the chest of the person who is reclining next to you. In this position, exchanging comments, even whispered words, would be quite simple (for example, John

13:21-25). Understanding a reclining meal eases our understanding of the woman who anointed the feet of Jesus with her tears and dried them with her hair as he ate at another banquet (Luke 7:36-50). The woman was not crawling around under a table as we might imagine. Instead, she was kneeling at the feet of Jesus as those feet were outstretched from the center table. Three very significant things took place at this special meal.

Washing
the Disciples' Feet ■

Read Genesis 18:4; 19:2; 43:24; Luke 7:44. How was footwashing a part of biblical hospitality? In spite of this gesture being one of respect, it was too humble a task for the host.

Read John 13:1-20. What did Jesus do? What did it mean that Jesus would be willing, even insist, that he should wash the feet of his disciples; persons who in that society would have been considered "under" their master?

What does this role reversal mean for all disciples of Jesus Christ? Peter objected; what did he seem to be thinking about Jesus' offer to wash him? How would you feel if the pastor offered to wash your feet? How does participating in this ritual give Peter and the disciples "a part of Jesus"? What does it mean in practical terms today to "do as I [Jesus] have done to you"?

Washing the Disciples' Feet

Only the Gospel of John reports that while the followers of Jesus were still eating, Jesus, the host for the meal, arose from the table, laid aside his garment, and wrapped a towel around his waist. Then he poured water into a basin and knelt silently at the feet of each assembled there, gently washing from his guest's feet the grime from a day's tramp through Jerusalem (John 13:1-20).

Footwashing, a common practice in the Mediterranean area at the time, was an act of personal hygiene and an act of hospitality. As an act of hospitality, footwashing was a means of welcoming a guest. The guest was offered water to wash his own feet (see, for example, Genesis 18:4; 19:2; 43:24; and Luke 7:44), or his feet were washed by a servant of the host.

But when Jesus arose from table, girded himself with a towel, and took up a basin of water, he was uniquely combining the functions of both host and servant. That he as the group's teacher and leader was host for the meal is unquestionable. But in the act of shedding his own garment and putting the towel around his middle, Jesus was adopting the role of a servant. Capture the point here: The host is the servant; the leader leads by serving; the definition of leadership is humble service.

Reenact your own foot-washing. Have a basin, water, wash cloth, and towels available and take turns washing the feet of those who are willing to participate.

How did it feel to wash another's feet? to have your feet washed? If you did not participate (Peter's first impulse), why not? How did it feel to be "on the outside" of this act?

Peter, perhaps speaking for all of the disciples, asks if Jesus is going to wash his, Peter's, feet. Jesus' response is enigmatic (see John 13:7). Peter recoils at the thought of Jesus washing his feet; imagine Peter drawing his feet up under his body as he reclines at the table. Jesus indicates that unless Peter is willing to participate and fellowship with Jesus fully, Peter can have no part of Jesus (John 13:8).

Peter still does not comprehend; he begs to be washed all over, as if the power of the action is in the water. But as Jesus responds in verse 10, the power of the symbolism is not in the cleansing water but in the relationship with Jesus the Christ. In other words, the footwashing (and the body washing Peter requests) is not a purification rite; instead it is a symbol of the relationship that God offers to all through Jesus the Christ.

But the lesson is not yet complete. Jesus demands a similar kind of servant leadership from his followers. "So if I, your Lord and Teacher have washed your feet, you also ought to wash one another's feet. For I have set you an example, that you also should do as I have done to you" (John 13:14-15). Jesus is calling not just for the servant leadership symbolized by the footwashing, but also for the kind of self-giving relationship among his followers that he has modeled for them.

Predicting His Betrayal ■

Read the four Gospel accounts of the prediction of Jesus' betrayal. Then look at John's version (13:21-30).

Have a slip of paper for each member of the group.

Predicting His Betrayal

Just as Jesus interrupted this special meal by washing the feet of his followers, he interrupted it a second time: "Truly I tell you, one of you will betray me (Matthew 26:21b; Mark 14:18; John 13:21).

The disciples were greatly distressed, troubled, perplexed (Matthew 26:22; Mark 14:19). Perhaps, they may have thought, he

On one of them write, *Judas*; on another, *Peter*, on another, *Narrator*; and on the rest, *Disciple*. Select a Jesus to pass out the slips. **Be sure Jesus, knows who Judas is. (If the paper slips are different colors, that would help.)** The narrator will start. Try to recreate this scene as you read the account in John 13—the upset, the confusion, occasions when all are speaking at once. Then discuss the experience. Ask *Judas* how it felt to be tagged as the betrayer; how *Jesus* felt to announce a friend as a betrayer; how *Peter* and the other *disciples* felt to discover one of their company to be a traitor.

What insights came to you with this reenactment that you had missed before?

was using the word *you* in a very broad sense, not meaning "those of us here now." But as if to anchor his point, Matthew and Mark report that Jesus indicated that the betrayer was one who was even then dipping his hand into the same bowl from which Jesus was eating. That meant that the betrayer was right there, reclining around the table with them, that the betrayer was one of those who made up the inner circle (Matthew 26:23; Mark 14:20).

The Gospel of John reports that Jesus directly identified the betrayer (John 13:23-26; Matthew's account does so also, but perhaps less obviously—Matthew 26:25). Notice the interplay in John's account. All the disciples were questioning who the betrayer might be. Peter, who is reclining at a bit of a distance from Jesus, motions to the disciple reclining in front of Jesus. This disciple is identified as "the one whom Jesus loved" (John 13:23), often thought to be the apostle John.

Picture John, then, leaning back onto the chest of Jesus and whispering, "Lord, who is it?" (John 13:25). Jesus does not avoid the question but instead tells John that he, Jesus, will dip a piece of bread into the bowl, then hand it to the betrayer. Imagine how closely John followed this action—first, Jesus breaking off a piece of bread, then dipping it into the bowl, then purposefully handing it to Judas Iscariot (John 13:26). Did John, Peter, and we catch the significance of the signal? Jesus extended a symbol of friendship and hospitality, a morsel of food, even to the one Jesus knew would betray him.

The Lord's Supper

Read the accounts of the Last Supper. What are the key active words in this rit-

Institution of the Lord's Supper

The third major event that took place in that room that night was what we observe and celebrate as the Lord's Supper. While

ual? What does it mean to do this "in remembrance"? What did Jesus mean about his blood being "poured out"?

the Gospel of John does not speak of the Lord's Supper as such, Paul knew well of it and described it in detail (1 Corinthians 11:23-26). The Synoptic Gospels agree closely in their descriptions of the Lord's Supper (Matthew 26:26-29; Mark 14:22-25; and Luke 22:15-20).

The action is simple. Jesus takes bread, blesses it, breaks it, and passes it to his disciples with the instruction to eat it, for it is his body. Luke adds, "Do this in remembrance of me" (Luke 22:19b). While Luke omits the specific reference in Matthew and Mark to the blessing of the cup, the three Synoptic Gospels agree that Jesus instructed his disciples to drink from the cup, referring directly to its contents as his blood "poured out" (in all three Gospels) for many ("you" in Luke's Gospel).

What was the nature of the covenant Jesus established with his disciples? What is your part in that covenant? God's part? What does that mean for us? for you? What is the most difficult aspect for you in keeping the covenant? the easiest?

Pay particular attention to a key word that Jesus uses in all three descriptions of this event. That word is *covenant*. Throughout the Scriptures, a meal, eating and drinking together, is the seal of a covenant between parties. (This custom continues to this day when major contracts are often celebrated by both sides with food and drink.) Thus, Jesus was reminding his disciples that he was doing more than asking them to remember him each time they ate and drank—although that is certainly a dimension of the Lord's Supper. He was at the same time describing and enacting a new covenant between the disciples and himself as a symbol for the new covenant between God and humankind.

Covenant

A covenant is an everlasting relationship between two parties; it is far more than a legal contract or an agreement that is completed at a certain time. The covenants that God had with God's people as described in the Hebrew Scriptures had been breached and violated time and again by the people. But Jesus is pointing out that the new covenant, the one being made this night and in the days to follow, is an everlasting covenant; for it will be sealed not with the ordinary food of humankind, but with the very flesh and blood of the Word become flesh. It is a covenant of grace and forgiveness for all of God's people, not just those who considered themselves the chosen people.

The amazing part of this covenant is that (at least in the Synoptic accounts) the traitor, the betrayer Judas, was still at the table with Jesus. John 13:21-30 indicates that Judas left as soon as the betrayal was predicted. Luke positions the announcement of the betrayal after the institution of the Lord's Supper. Still, the implication is clear that Judas participated in the Lord's Supper, even as we who are sinful today are invited to participate in the Lord's Supper.

Closing Prayer ■

At the conclusion of your session, invite your pastor to serve Communion to the group. If he or she is not available, ask the pastor to consecrate the elements, and then have a lay person distribute them. Use one or more hymns that either have to do with Communion or with Maundy Thursday. Close with a prayer of confession and pardon for the many ways we betray Jesus Christ and fail in our covenant. Take time in prayer to consider that covenant and to make or renew your commitment to Jesus Christ.

The Lord's Supper, as instituted that fateful night, was a many-faceted and multi-dimensional reality. It remains so to this day. "When they had sung the hymn, they went out to the Mount of Olives" (Matthew 26:30; Mark 14:26); "He ... went ... to the Mount of Olives; and his disciples followed him" (Luke 22:39). Events were hastening to a terrible conclusion.

Session Four

Arrest

Session Focus ■

This session focuses on the arrest of Jesus and the key persons who enabled the arrest to take place.

Session Objective ■

You will explore the person and character of Judas and his collusion with the Jewish authorities and better understand the dynamics of the betrayal and its aftermath.

Session Preparation ■

Have on hand the Gospel parallel, a map of the city of Jerusalem and surrounding area, and several copies of your denomination's hymnal.

Choose from among these activities and discussion starters to plan your lesson.

What Is to Take Place ■

On the map of Jerusalem locate the East Gate, the Kidron Valley, and the Mount of Olives. The Mount of Olives has an elevation of about 2,700 feet, so Jesus and his party could well have had an

The evening meal was over; Jesus and the disciples had sung a hymn (possibly from Psalms 115–118, the psalms for this holy day); and then they made their way to the Mount of Olives, perhaps to spend this night as they may have done other nights during this holy week.

What Is to Take Place

The journey to the Mount of Olives was not difficult; they had walked it many times. Most likely, they exited from the city by the Eastern Gate. Then they followed a steep path down into the Kidron Valley and up the other side of the valley to the Mount of Olives. According to Matthew and Mark, while they were walking down into the valley and up the other side Jesus said, "You will all become deserters." Imagine the impact that statement must have had on those who followed the man Jesus. He went on, "For it is written, 'I will strike the shepherd, and the sheep of the flock will be scattered.'" But then followed perhaps a most puzzling statement: "But after I am raised up, I will go ahead of you to Galilee" (Matthew 26:30-32; Mark 14:26-28). Notice what Jesus was doing with these statements:

First, he was indicating that the faith of the followers was not yet sufficiently strong to resist the temptation to save their own lives, even though it be at the cost of his

excellent view of the city in the daylight and of persons approaching the top of the Mount by torchlight.

Read Matthew 26:30-32 and Mark 14:26-28 (using the Gospel parallel, if you have it). Form three groups and assign to each group one of three paragraphs ("First . . . , Second. . . , Third . . .") in the main text that refers to what Jesus was doing with the "betrayal" statement.

What is the key point in each of these assessments? What does the related Scripture, if cited, add to your understanding of what Jesus meant and said? of what the disciples must have been thinking or doing?

Read Jesus' prediction of Peter's denial. Peter usually gets more attention than the other disciples for his denial, but Jesus predicted that *all* the disciples would desert him—and they did. Peter said he would never fall away, and the others agreed—but they all did. Is Peter's denial any different or any worse than Judas's betrayal or the disciples' desertion? Did any of Jesus' followers acquit themselves well that evening? Do you relate to any of the disciples in this event? Why? How?

life. As it is now, the word *deserters* was a repugnant term then. Jesus was not being gentle with his disciples; he knew what was ahead, and he knew they lacked the courage to see through to the end what had been planned.

Second, he was building his case on prophecy. The scattering of the sheep at the death of the shepherd is part of Zechariah 13:7-9, in many ways a suffering servant song similar to Isaiah 53. Did the disciples still fail to see that Jesus was fulfilling significant dimensions of Hebrew Scripture prophecy; were they so dense that Jesus must repeatedly point it out to them? Perhaps Jesus' purpose here, as in so many of his other statements, was to be sure that no one missed the point, that no doubt could remain. He is the Messiah as promised by the prophets, but his messiahship is far different from what the popular culture had assumed it was to be.

Third, Jesus promised that after his death, his disciples would see him in Galilee. The significance of this, quite apart from the promise of the Resurrection, "after I am raised up" (Matthew 26:32; Mark 14:28), is that the resurrected Christ is not localized in Jerusalem. The Christ is the Christ of all persons everywhere, no longer bound by the Temple or by the law, but free to be where God's people are, wherever that might be.

Did the disciples comprehend all of this? Probably not, if Peter's response is indicative of the other disciples. Peter protests that even though the others desert Jesus, he never would. (Note that the others agree.) And Jesus offers the sad prediction that surely Peter will deny Jesus three times before morning light (Matthew 26:34-35; Mark 14:29-31; see Luke 22:31-34).

It had been a sad evening for Peter. He misunderstood the washing of the disciples' feet at the dinner, he fretted about who was going to betray Jesus, and now Jesus was saying that despite his very best intentions, he (Peter) would desert him. Always impetuous, Peter argued with Jesus—Mark's Gospel says "vehemently"—to indicate his willingness to go to the very end with Jesus, whatever that end might be.

The Garden Prayer

The Garden Prayer ■

Read the parallel accounts of Jesus in the garden to recall what happened there. Look up these garden references in the Scripture index in your hymnal. Are any hymns, such as "I Stand Amazed in the Presence," based on the Garden scene? (Sing or read the hymn together.) What do the lyrics (and the Scriptures) say about Jesus? about what his time in prayer means for all of his followers? about our own "garden moments" in our relationship to Jesus Christ?

By now the group had arrived at the Mount of Olives at a place called Gethsemane. Gethsemane is often called a garden; but most likely, Gethsemane was a small grove of olive trees and perhaps a few fruit or berry trees.

Jesus asked his followers to wait for him on the edge of the grove, then he took with him three of his closest apostles and asked them to wait and watch with him while he prayed (Matthew 26:36-46; Mark 14:32-42; Luke 22:40-46). His face was lined with grief; no longer relaxed and calm, Jesus was, to use the words of Matthew and Mark, "agitated." Why did he ask these three apostles to watch and wait with him? Was the man Jesus frightened about what was to take place? Was he questioning his own ability to see through to the end the task God had given him? Was he concerned for his followers, as he indicated in his high priestly prayer at the supper just a short time before (John 17:6-19)?

Jesus prayed that God might prevent what was about to take place, not submit him to the awful trial ahead; remove the cup (a symbol for that of which he was about to partake). But note the words of Jesus that immediately followed this plea: "Yet not what I want but what you want" (Matthew 26:39;

Identify the main features of this time in the garden: the prayer, the action of the disciples, Jesus' response to them. How do you understand Jesus' prayer: "Let this pass, but your will be done"? (Remember that Jesus had predicted great violence against himself.) How do you respond to the three sleeping disciples and their inattention?

Mark 14:36) and "not my will but yours be done" (Luke 22:42). After offering this prayer amid grief and agitation that resulted in profuse perspiration (Luke 22:44), Jesus arose and returned to the three disciples. He found them asleep.

Our first reaction might be to criticize their inattention. Yet, the apostles still did not understand fully what was happening; they had just consumed a very large, festival meal; and they had been "on the go" since arriving in Jerusalem on Sunday. They were exhausted; Jesus himself was probably operating on what we often call nervous energy. These disciples were being very human, and no doubt Jesus understood this even as he gently chided them (Matthew 26:40-41; Mark 14:37-38; Luke 22:46).

Mark and Matthew report that this same scenario took place three times; each time Jesus praying that he would not have to endure the ordeal ahead of him, but each time affirming that God's will would be done. Each time Jesus returned to his followers to find them sleeping, "for their eyes were heavy" (Matthew 26:43; Mark 14:40). The third time he came to the disciples, his message was a bit different: "Get up, let us be going. See, my betrayer is at hand" (Matthew 26:46; Mark 14:42).

Invite volunteers to retell the story from the point of view of Jesus, of one who accompanied him, and of one of the rest of the disciples who stayed still further off. What insights come to mind from looking at the same story from different angles?

The phrase, "let us be going" can be misunderstood. Jesus is not speaking here of flight; he is not suggesting that he and the disciples try to escape. Jesus has already committed himself in prayer three different times to going through the task placed before him. Escape nor flight is not on his mind; to run away or to avoid this confrontation is not a part of Jesus at this moment. Perhaps the "let us be going" is an indication of his willingness to go see the coming events unfold.

Jesus had seen the arresting party approaching. No doubt he had watched as the crowd made its way by torchlight (John 18:3) down through the Kidron Valley and up the very same pathway on the Mount of Olives that he and his followers had taken only a few moments before. Leading the mob, the crowd with swords and clubs, was the disciple Judas.

Who Was Judas?

Who Was Judas? ■

Before you look any further at the Scriptures, brainstorm and list what you know about Judas and how you feel about his betrayal. Note what you think his motive was and the aftermath of his decision. Who else was involved? Keep the list on hand, and add to it as your exploration continues.

Surely one of the most complex and controversial characters in the world's history is the man Judas; surely as many legends and stories have arisen around this man as have almost any other character that has affected the lives of many other persons. Judas has been vilified and praised, excused as a puppet, and pilloried as the epitome of evil.

In truth, the Scriptures tell us very little about this man; and attractive as many of the stories and legends that surround him might be, we must limit our knowledge of him to that which is disclosed in the Gospels and in the Book of Acts.

His surname, Iscariot, may have suggested that he was from the town of Kerioth, a village in Judea. If this is true, then Judas was the only one of the twelve disciples who was from Judea rather than Galilee. As was mentioned earlier, a few scholars suggest that Judas was one of the radical *sicarii*, dagger-wielding zealots, although they may not have appeared on the Palestinian scene until around the mid-first century, after the Crucifixion. A few other scholars suggest that he was of the tribe of Issachar.

Perhaps all that can be said with certainty is that the name *Judas* was a common name of the time (another of the disciples of Jesus was named Judas, and at least seven other persons named Judas are mentioned in the Scriptures) and that the name *Iscariot* was used consistently to identify this Judas from the rest.

The Judas of the Bible ■

Divide all these identifying statements about Judas among the group members. Look up at least one or two of the Scriptures that support each statement.

Add information to the "Who Was Judas?" list and keep it in mind for the next activity. What did you learn? Did the Scripture references correct anything that you had recalled inaccurately? Now what overall portrait of Judas emerges?

The Judas of the Bible

- *Judas was one of the original twelve disciples (Matthew 10:4; Mark 3:19; Luke 6:16; John 6:71; Acts 1:15-17).*
- *Judas was treasurer of the band of apostles, probably a somewhat privileged position (John 12:6b; 13:29).*
- *Judas was a thief (John 12:6a). Was Judas recognized as a thief after the betrayal when his identity was hopelessly and forever tarnished? Or did the other disciples know all along? Would the disciples have consented to Judas carrying the common purse had they known he was a thief?*
- *Judas initiated the betrayal of Jesus (Matthew 26:14-16; Mark 14:10-11; Luke 22:3-6). Judas went to the chief priests and offered to betray Jesus for money. The Gospels do not indicate in any way that the chief priests and others sought out Judas or any of the other disciples in hopes of finding one who would betray Jesus.*
- *Jesus knew of Judas's betrayal in advance, at least as early as the festival meal that night (Matthew 26:20-25; Mark 14:17-21; Luke 22:14, 21-23; John 13:21-30) and most probably much earlier than that.*
- *Judas betrayed Jesus with a kiss (Matthew 26:48-49; Mark 14:44-45; Luke 22:47-48). Men kissing men was not at all unusual in the culture of first-century Judea, just as it is a common custom in many parts of the world today. But to use this loving and intimate greeting as a means of marking one for death is an ultimate betrayal. Perhaps some*

in the group of disciples that night—and perhaps even some in the arresting crowd—recalled the story of Joab's brutal murder of Amasa under the guise of a welcoming kiss (2 Samuel 20:4-10a).

- *Judas died a miserable death. Matthew reports that Judas repented and sought to return the money to the chief priests, then hanged himself (Matthew 27:3-10). Luke, the writer of the Book of Acts, indicates that Judas bought a field with the proceeds of the betrayal and there suffered a gruesome death (Acts 1:18).*

Judas and the Betrayal ■

Look at the possible motivations Judas may have had. Work individually, or form seven small groups and divide the list of possible motivations (the **bold text**). Spend a few minutes discussing the merits of the motive; then bring everyone together to debate. After the presentation of all arguments, decide, based on the discussion and all the Scripture references about Judas and his character, what seems to be the plausible motive. (This does not necessarily make it accurate; Scripture does not always clearly disclose these answers.)

Judas and the Betrayal

Did Judas betray Jesus unto death? Or did Judas merely agree to tell the chief priests where they might find Jesus in a place apart from the city and thus well away from a potential riot? Many scholars believe that the latter is the more likely reality. Judas knew where Jesus would go following the supper, and he knew that the quiet grove of olive and fruit trees at Gethsemane would not attract a crowd and would probably not encourage the followers of Jesus to put up an armed struggle.

But the larger question has always been: Why did Judas betray Jesus? A simple answer is that **Judas betrayed Jesus for the money** that was offered. However, this seems unlikely. Only Matthew mentions the amount, and Judas indicated his willingness before negotiating the price. The amount of money was not that much in real terms—the wage of a shepherd or the price of an injured slave—and to betray someone with whom one had lived intimately for three years for such a paltry sum seems unlikely.

Another argument is that **Judas believed that Jesus was truly planning to die for the people, and Judas just assisted** Jesus in this process. Scriptural evidence for this is Mark 14:3-11. Put Judas's thinking this way: "If Jesus is going to die anyway, why not make a bit of a profit from it?" Some have suggested that Judas betrayed Jesus in order to help Jesus fulfill his purpose by dying; but Mark 14:21 would seem to argue against this.

Perhaps, say some, **Judas was originally a very pious Jew who recoiled at Jesus' seeming indifference to the law** and willful disobedience of such regulations as the sabbath ordinances. But had that been the case, Judas could have simply walked away from Jesus and the band of the disciples, as many had already done (John 6:60-66). Betrayal was not necessary.

Or, as a few others have suggested, did **Judas become convinced over a period of time that Jesus was in reality a false messiah** who was deceiving the people? According to the law, such a person must be executed, even a family member or "your most intimate friend" (Deuteronomy 13:1-11).

Was Judas part of a divine plan, a puppet in the hands of God, chosen from the very beginning to assume the role of the greatest villain in history? If so, would Jesus have been aware of this, and if he were, would Jesus have made the "woe to you" statement recorded in Mark 14:21? If Judas had been part of God's divine plan, would God have allowed the horrible death of Judas (who had completed the assigned task) as described in Acts 1:18?

Was Judas a puppet in the hands of Satan? Luke 22:3-4 says that Satan entered into Judas, and *then* Judas sought out the religious officials and plotted with them. Elsewhere, Jesus had said to Peter that Satan was pushing him to say or do things that he (Peter, who is not characterized as a villain) either didn't mean or would regret (Matthew 16:22-23; Mark 8:32-33). Was Judas acting not on his own power, but under the control of the evil one?

Was Judas acting of his own free will, choosing to betray Jesus in order to stimulate an armed uprising against the Romans? Some who try to argue that Judas was a zealot take this position, but it is not soundly based in Scripture. Whether or not he was a zealot, a case can be made for Judas acting on his own will, for if he had not, would he have repented, tried to return the money, then hanged himself, as Matthew reports?

Perhaps two very tentative conclusions can be reached. First, the stories about Judas in the Gospels were written long after the events they describe. Decades of hatred toward Judas had passed before the Gospels were committed to writing. In the formative years of the Christian movement, Judas was quite understandably portrayed as the most evil of persons, fully deserving of the consequences of his actions. The somewhat sophisticated ways we view Judas theologically in our time were unknown to the Gospel writers. Therefore, Judas is described in the Scriptures always and only as a villain with no attempt to probe the causes for his actions.

Second, we may never know the myriad of reasons Judas chose to take the action he did. Had Judas not taken that action, would Jesus still have gone to the cross? Probably. Is Judas alone to blame for the execution of Jesus? Probably not, for many forces were

What was your conclusion? How did you arrive at your conclusion? Was there more than one strong opinion or argument for different motivations? Any suggestion of a motive that was not presented in the text? Have our religious history and texts given a fair report of Judas? Explain.

arrayed against the man from Galilee; and, by his own reckoning, time was running out.

Judas remains one of history's—and faith's—greatest enigmas.

Captured

Captured ■

The Gospel accounts give a fairly terse report of the events of the arrest. Read the different versions and then retell the story. Start with one person who will begin with the arrival of Judas and who will add detail and "color" to the biblical account, based on what we know of the whole story, of the main characters, and human nature. After a paragraph or two, the second person will continue the story in like manner, and so on until group members finish the episode. Consider the noise, the confusion, the high emotional state, the use of violence, the dark, the "unholy alliances" of priest and Roman, and so on.

Now what picture emerges? What sights, sounds, smells, touch or texture, and tastes came to mind? what feelings and attitudes? what reactions? How does this retelling bring you personally into the events? Do you relate to anyone present? If so, how might Jesus have felt about you, had you been there?

The mob arrived. Judas had given his sign; the mob identified Jesus as the one they wanted; and they surrounded him, preventing escape (Matthew 26:47-56; Mark 14:43-52; Luke 22:47-53; John 18:2-11). In a moment of courage, one of the followers of Jesus drew a sword and slashed out. His sword found the ear of a slave of the high priest and severed it. Jesus' response was predictable; Luke reports that he healed the man's ear with a touch while at the same time halting further armed resistance (Luke 22:49-51). Matthew supports this position, and quotes Jesus as claiming that he could summon twelve legions of angels to defend him, should he choose (Matthew 26:53).

The Gospel of John reveals a poignant episode in the grove of olive trees that is not mentioned in the Synoptic Gospels. Consistent with the high priestly prayer in John 17, Jesus pleads for his followers (John 18:4-9). Jesus readily identifies himself as the one the mob is seeking; he surrenders, as it were to the mob, and entreats them to let his followers go free. Jesus is ready to carry out the awesome responsibility that God has placed upon him, but he is careful not to involve his followers in the same awful fate.

Interestingly, John's Gospel identifies the attacking swordsman as Peter (John 18:10). This is not too surprising considering Peter's repeated impetuousness. John also identifies the servant as Malchus. As Malchus is a Nabatean name, is John attempting to hint at the inclusiveness of the Gospel at this point, that is, that all persons, Jew and Gentile alike, are brought into the sphere of Jesus' influence?

"Why Like This?"

Jesus is not finished with the mob yet. We might surmise that Jesus looked over the mob and saw there some of the chief priests, elders, and Pharisees, perhaps all members of the Sanhedrin. Also in attendance were Temple police, probably Levites whose duties involved maintaining order in the Temple area. Did these Temple police recall Jesus' rage in the Temple earlier in the week? We do not know.

We might also surmise that the mob included ordinary people of Jerusalem. We can imagine ordinary folks seeing a procession going by, torches held aloft, spears, swords, and clubs at the ready, walking briskly toward a gate in the walls of the city. No doubt some of these folks joined the mob, falling in behind the more formal members of the arresting group. While the ordinary citizens of Jerusalem are separated from us by two millennia, they were probably very much like we are—curious and eager to find out what's going on.

Consider John's Gospel again. Only John reports a detachment of soldiers in the arresting crowd (John 18:3). Since John reports soldiers "together with police from the chief priests and the Pharisees," that is, Temple police, then the power of Rome was involved and actively participating in the arrest of the man in the olive grove. The detachment of Roman soldiers lent more than simply armed might to the crowd. They conferred on the arresting mob a legitimacy, an authority the crowd could not have claimed otherwise. Note the two groups represented in the

"Why Like This?" ■

Do a journalling exercise. Reflect on the question, "Why like this?" Choose at least two different points of view: that of one of the major participants or the onlookers, and yourself, as if you had been there.

Consider the presence of Temple police, Roman soldiers, a disciple who had betrayed his master, the other befuddled disciples and the general chaos, the implications of certain groups of people working together (Pharisees and Roman authorities, for example), the apparent calm of Jesus, and his logical question: Why have you come after me as if I were a bandit?

Compare journal entries among those who wish to share.

arresting mob: the religious power, in the persons of those Sanhedrin members who made the trek across the Kidron Valley; and the secular power, in the persons of the Roman soldiers reported by John.

What was the response of Jesus, the man they were seeking, to this arresting mob? The three Synoptic Gospels are remarkably similar at this point. Matthew says, "At that hour Jesus said to the crowds, 'Have you come out with swords and clubs to arrest me as though I were a bandit? Day after day I sat in the temple teaching, and you did not arrest me' " (Matthew 26:55; see also Mark 14:48 and Luke 22:52-53). In effect, Jesus is asking, Why? Why the swords and clubs? Why the soldiers and the Temple police? Why the lanterns and the torches? Why the commotion?

In Matthew and in Luke, Jesus answers his own question, but in two different ways. Matthew, always seeking to demonstrate that Jesus was the fulfillment of Old Testament prophecy, quotes Jesus as saying, "But all this has taken place, so that the scriptures of the prophets may be fulfilled" (26:56). Jesus may not be making reference to a particular Scripture in this case, but rather making a general reference to passages such as Psalms 22, 69, and Isaiah 53. Luke, writing to a predominantly Gentile audience, cites Jesus remarking, "But this is your hour, and the power of darkness" (Luke 22:53b).

Both accounts provide information from the individual writers. Evil was afoot in the world that night, and for a time the powers of evil had ascendancy. That this would transpire had been predicted in the prophecies of the Hebrew Scriptures. Thus, the Gospels of Luke and Matthew are not in conflict but rather are complementary.

What does it add to your understanding of these events to consider that everything was done in order to fulfill the Scriptures? Does this mean that everything was predetermined? inevitable? irrevocable? something else? Explain.

The Disciples Desert Him ■

The detachment of armed soldiers should have been able to contain and arrest all, or at least some, of the disciples, but didn't. Were the disciples really in danger, do you think? Was it necessary to flee? (Remember that events look very different in retrospect than they do in the heat of the moment.)

Closing Prayer ■

As a private exercise, think about all your opportunities to love and serve Christ that you have ignored or from which you have fled. How have you deserted God at critical moments? What have you done to return?

Offer prayers of strength for all believers who waver. Consider your commitment to Jesus Christ, and take time in prayer to make or renew your covenant to love and serve him without fear.

"The Disciples Deserted Him and Fled"

What transpired next is unclear. Mark tells the curious story of the young man who literally ran out of his garment when the mob tried to take hold of him (Mark 14:51). Tradition claims that this young man was Mark, the writer of this Gospel, and that the inclusion of this story served to give credibility to the account. But this is conjecture; no one can say for certain just who this young man was or why his story is included in Mark's Gospel.

But what happened to Jesus in these moments? He did not put up a struggle or try to escape. Only John reports that he was bound (18:12). Did the mob strike him? Guard him at sword's point? Hurl insults at him? We simply do not know. Quite likely the mob surrounded him and shouted orders to him to move along with them. But the Gospel writers, so often masters of understatement, do not dwell on such details. Jesus was arrested and led back to the city as a criminal.

However, one more thing took place during those terrible moments in the grove of olive trees. The prediction Jesus made only a few moments earlier in the olive grove, came frighteningly true. Jesus had said that all of his closest followers would leave, disappear, become as scattered sheep once the shepherd had been stricken (Matthew 26:31; Mark 14:27). Now, again in classic understatement, Matthew and Mark relate one of the saddest verses in the Scriptures: "Then all the disciples deserted him and fled (Matthew 26:56b; Mark 14:50).

Session Five

Trial

Jesus was alone. The arresting party had him in its power; his disciples had forsaken him and fled. Surrounded by the Temple police, soldiers, and other members of this group, Jesus was escorted back down the Kidron Valley, up the western slope, and into the city of Jerusalem.

Back in Jerusalem

The destination? The Synoptic Gospels are clear: The arresting party was escorting Jesus to the house of Caiaphas, the high priest (Matthew 26:57; Mark 14:53; Luke 22:54). John (18:13) suggests that they took Jesus first to Annas, the father-in-law of Caiaphas.

Scholars have argued about this discrepancy for centuries without satisfactory results. Annas probably preceded Caiaphas as high priest, most likely appointed by the Roman Quirinius about A.D. 6 or 7, but removed from office by Valerius Gratus about ten years later. Even though removed from office by the Roman officials, Annas would still have had considerable influence in Jerusalem. Annas was probably a member of the Sanhedrin.

Some of the simplest resolutions of this inconsistency are the most satisfactory. For example, could Annas and Caiaphas have been in the same house that evening? It was the First Day of Unleavened Bread, a family

Session Focus ■
This session focuses on the trial of Jesus and the key persons who enabled the trial to take place.

Session Objective ■
You will explore the person and character of Pilate, Caiaphas, and the crowd as well as the some of the workings of the Jewish legal system to better understand the trial.

Session Preparation ■
Have on hand the Gospel parallel, a map of Jerusalem during Jesus' ministry from a Bible atlas or study Bible, and a Bible dictionary.

Choose from among these activities and discussion starters to plan your lesson.

Back in Jerusalem ■
Begin your reading of these Holy Week events by looking up Matthew 26:57; Mark 14:53; Luke 22:54; John 18:13. Use the Gospel parallel if you have one.

Apparently the chief priest, Caiaphas, had sent his people to detain Jesus and was waiting at home for him (see Matthew 26:47, for example).

Try to imagine the atmosphere that greeted Jesus' arrival. What, do you think, was the mood? Who was there?

The House of Caiaphas ■

Look at a map of Jerusalem to locate the house of Caia-phas in relation to the Temple and to the Golden (or eastern) Gate. How far was Jesus dragged from the Mount of Olives?

Again, try to immerse your senses in the mood of the event as if you were one of the crowd; one of the disciples; Jesus; a Jewish leader waiting at Caiaphas's house.

Who Was There? ■

The following several activities delve into those persons likely to have had a

festival and meal. If Annas had been in Caiaphas's home, he may indeed have seen Jesus before Caiaphas did. John 18:24 does not necessarily contradict this. That Annas sent Jesus bound to Caiaphas does not mean that Annas literally sent Jesus a considerable distance, as to another house or another party of the city; it could simply mean that Annas turned Jesus over to Caiaphas.

The House of Caiaphas

According to tradition, the house of Caiaphas was in the southwest quadrant of the walled city of Jerusalem. The Golden Gate or eastern gate through which Jesus and the mob probably came was in the northeast quadrant of the city. If the tradition concerning Caiaphas's house is accurate, then the mob escorted Jesus in what amounted to a diagonal direction, northeast to southwest, through the major part of the city.

Imagination suggests that this was quite a procession. Soldiers; Temple police; shouting members of the mob carrying torches, swords, clubs, all rather late in the evening of the First Day of Unleavened Bread when homes would be filled with people celebrating the festival. Did people run to see the cause of the commotion in the narrow, winding streets? Did they fall in behind the procession to discover what was happening? Did they wonder about the man in the middle of the mob, the one who was bound, the key figure in this strange and awful procession? Finally, the procession arrived at the house of Caiaphas.

Who Was There?

Who was present in the house of Caiaphas that night? Again, certainty is impossible, but some general suggestions might be made.

part in the preliminary
questioning of Jesus.
Consider assigning parts to
various group members and
reenacting that scene to
get a sense of the mood
and how Jesus may have
experienced it himself.

Caiaphas ■

Who was Caiaphas? What
was he like? How did he
"fit" with the Roman
authorities? How might
Jesus have anticipated
being treated by Caiaphas?

Bible 301
The Sanhedrin □

Using a Bible dictionary,
look up Sanhedrin. What
was the membership and
function of the Sanhedrin?
What was the limit of the
members' power? If this

Caiaphas

Surely, Caiaphas himself was there.
Caiaphas was high priest, appointed to that
role by Valerius Gratus when this Roman
official deposed Annas as high priest. The
date is uncertain, but most authorities suggest that Caiaphas was appointed to the high
priesthood about A.D. 17 or 18. Records indicate that Caiaphas served in this role until he
was removed from office by the Roman
procurator Vitellis about A.D. 36 or 37; a
rather long term of office at that time.

Note, too, that because the office of high
priest was filled by appointment by Roman
officials, Caiaphas must have been on good
terms with the Roman officials who ruled
Judea at the time, including the governor
Pontius Pilate. The Roman administrator
had life and death power over the Judeans;
thus, a Roman ruler could have easily
removed from office a trouble-making high
priest.

Can we conclude, then, that Caiaphas
must have been a clever politician, able to
please his Roman masters while at the same
time keeping the Jewish populace in check
by serving the duties of the high priesthood
in a manner satisfactory to them? Caiaphas
was probably a Saduccee, an aristocrat, personally wealthy, intent on maintaining order,
and respected in the Sanhedrin, of which he
was president. He had immense power over
the Jewish prisoner Jesus, now brought
before him.

Members of the Sanhedrin

The Gospel records are not clear on who
else was present in the house of Caiaphas
that night. Quite probably, a number of the
members of the Sanhedrin were present, but
the gathering was almost certainly not a for-

gathering were not a full meeting, what legitimate business could they conduct?

mal meeting of the Sanhedrin. This was a feast day, it was late in the evening, the sabbath was fast approaching, and Sanhedrin members were concerned with many things now that the city was filled to overflowing with pilgrims. We cannot conclude that the case of Jesus was sufficiently important for Caiaphas to have called a special session of the Sanhedrin for that night any more than special middle-of-the-night sessions of the United States Congress are called for minor concerns (such as a wandering preacher would have been for the Sanhedrin). So, we might fairly assume that *some* of the chief priests, elders, and scribes were present in Caiaphas's house that night; but we cannot ascertain if these comprised even a simple majority of the Sanhedrin or if they attempted to act in any way as the formal body of the Sanhedrin.

The Witnesses

Look up these passages that refer to witnesses and their proper conduct: Deuteronomy 17:6-7; 19:15-21; Proverbs 21:28; Matthew 26:60-62. What role did the witnesses play in this inquiry? Was it done according to the law? What impact did their testimony have and what had to be done to get it?

Also present in the house that night were witnesses against Jesus. Again, who were they? We simply do not know; the Gospels do not tell us. How many were present? Again, the answer is unknown. Matthew and Mark speak of "many" (Matthew 26:60; Mark 14:56), but what constitutes "many"? And from where did these witnesses come? Were they recruited by Caiaphas and members of the Sanhedrin? Were they part of the arrest mob? Did they come when they heard about the meeting at Caiaphas's house? We simply do not know.

The Retinue

Read Matthew 26:69-75; Mark 14:66-72; Luke 22:54b-62. Who among this retinue recognized and

Also present in and around the house of Caiaphas that night were the usual retinue of servants, guards, Temple police, and household employees. John reports that various

questioned Peter? Did they have any power to hurt him? If so, how? Does that, do you think, justify Peter's denial?

Read or sing together stanzas 1–2 of "Ah, Holy Jesus" or stanza 2 of "O Sacred Head, Now Wounded." These lyrics imply that, like Peter, we can still deny Jesus Christ and send him to his crucifixion.

Do you have any sense of culpability for or participation in the betrayal or the Crucifixion? What do these lyrics mean to you personally? How do they shape or influence your faith? your relationship to God and Jesus Christ?

persons in this mixed group identified Peter from the olive grove (John 18:15-18; 25-27). It was with these persons that the disciple Peter sat and waited the outcome of what was transpiring in the house. It was these who challenged Peter as he sat by the fire, accusing him of being a follower of the man brought to Caiaphas's house. It was these who detected that Peter was from Galilee through his accent, much as we might be able to identify a person from the deep south of the United States; from Brooklyn, New York; or from some other areas, by a regional accent. It was before these people that Peter three times denied knowing Jesus, just as Jesus had predicted. And it was from these that Peter ran in shame and guilt, weeping bitterly (Matthew 26:69-75; Mark 14:66-72; Luke 22:54b-62).

Luke 22:61 is a difficult verse. Was Jesus standing in some position where he and Peter could literally see each other when Peter denied him? Or is the reference symbolic, such as we feel Christ watching us when we knowingly violate his love? Many scholars argue that the latter is more probable; that Peter felt the Lord looking at him, felt the presence of the Lord, and felt through that sense of presence his own shame and guilt for his betrayal. The fact that Luke uses the word *Lord* here rather than *Jesus* may add some credibility to the argument that the reference is symbolic rather than literal.

What Happened in the House?

We Christians do not know with certainty what transpired in the house of Caiaphas that night. Surely, no disciples of Jesus were present inside the house. (John 18:15-16 reports Peter and another disciple, probably

John, went as far as the courtyard, but not into the house itself.) No formal record of that meeting was ever made by the Sanhedrin members or by the Roman authorities. What we have are records written some thirty years after the fact; thus, they are not eyewitness accounts.

The Authorities Confer ■

Imagine yourselves as members of the Sanhedrin. Not all of your members are present. Some of you are Pharisees and are very precise about the letter of the law. Others are Sadducees and are very concerned about the status quo, especially with Rome. Confer together about what you are doing. How should you proceed? What can you legally decide and what is your reasoning?

The Authorities Confer

The Sanhedrin, sitting as an official body, had life and death power; it could execute persons who violated Jewish laws, although perhaps only with the permission of the Roman governor or procurator. This is apparent from Jospehus, from Philo, from the Jewish Mishnah, and most significantly, from the story of the stoning of Stephen (Acts 6–7). The somewhat confusing verse in John's Gospel that claims the Jews were not permitted to put anyone to death (John 18:31b) may be a reference to the fact that it was not a formal meeting of the Sanhedrin in Caiaphas's house, but instead of some members—chief priests, scribes, and elders. Such an informal group could not condemn someone to death any more than a group of persons in our time can condemn someone to death without a formal, legal trial.

So if the group in Caiaphas's house did not constitute an official meeting of the Sanhedrin, what were they doing? Their actions have been likened to the actions of a grand jury in our system. They were questioning Jesus to see if indeed he had violated the religious and political laws of the land to the extent that he should be tried on a capital charge (Matthew 26:57-68; Mark 14:53-65; Luke 22:54-54, 63-65).

False Testimony ■

Read Matthew 26:57-68;
Mark 14:53-65. What did
Jesus say about himself?
How did the authorities
react to it? How could his
response be considered
blasphemy?

False Testimony

The Scriptures report that many people gave false and confusing testimony until several witnesses indicated that Jesus had threatened to tear down the Temple, clearly an act of sedition. Then, in response to the questions of Caiaphas, Jesus "blasphemed" by claiming that he was the Messiah and that he would be seen on the right hand of God. Thus, the group in Caiaphas's house could accuse Jesus of sedition and of blasphemy, either of which was a capital offense at the time.

Here is where the Synoptic Gospels diverge slightly, but the variances are not cause for concern. Notice how Matthew and Mark suggest that this questioning of Jesus took place at night, *before* the cock crowed, announcing Peter's denials. Luke, however, indicates that the questioning took place *after* Peter's denials and *after* the cock crowed, that is, in the very early morning. In one scenario, the chief priests and others were assembled at night; in the scenario from Luke, they may not have assembled until dawn on Friday. This inconsistency may reflect a difference in understanding when a day began or ended—morning or evening.

Bible 301 ☐

Look up blasphemy in a
Bible dictionary. What is it
and what is the punishment
for it?

Now look up Son of Man.
How is this image used and
what does it mean? Why
might it elicit a negative
response from the religious
authorities?

If we follow the Matthew-Mark account, then all or part of the group from Caiaphas's house met again early Friday morning, perhaps reconsidered the evidence, and determined to send Jesus to Pilate (Matthew 27:1-2; Mark 15:1). If we follow Luke's account, the group met early Friday morning, interviewed Jesus very briefly, then concluded that they had enough evidence to send Jesus to Pilate (Luke 22:66–23:1). A middle of the night hearing or an early morning hearing; the sequence is not of crucial importance for the results were the same. Forward the prisoner, the man Jesus, to the Roman governor, Pontius Pilate.

Insults, Mocking, and Flogging

Insults, Mocking, and Flogging ■

Think about (but do not feel compelled to reveal or to discuss) the worst kind of pain you ever had to endure. What caused the pain? (an accident? illness? surgery? a fight? sports injury?) Knowing how it felt, would you ever volunteer to go through that pain—or the activity that led to it—again? Explain.

How does this memory help you understand Jesus' experience of being mocked and physically brutalized, especially since he knew it would be part of his ordeal—the "cup" that did not pass? What does it mean to you that Jesus did this willingly, as the Son of God and for the sake of humanity?

In either case, after the charges had been lodged and the determination made to take Jesus to Pilate, Jesus was physically and verbally abused, perhaps not directly by the chief priests, scribes, and elders, but certainly with their permission. Matthew and Mark suggest that those who offered the verdict (members of the council) participated in this abuse. The Temple police, the soldiers, and others spat upon him—an ultimate insult then as now—struck him, and mocked him. Mark reports that "the guards also took him over and beat him" (Mark 14:65b). If this refers to the guards at Caiaphas's house, to the Temple police, or to Roman soldiers the results are the same: a torturous, methodical, merciless, brutal beating by men who prided themselves on their efficiency in this regard.

Where did Jesus spend the night, either after the questioning by those gathered (Matthew and Mark) or before the dawn questioning (Luke)? Tradition suggests that Jesus was placed in a dungeon-like cave in or adjacent to Caiaphas's house. Pilgrims who visit the Church of St. Peter of Gallicantu (built over what is the traditional site of Caiaphas's palace) today are taken to this dungeon. It is a stone pit about twenty feet square with a stone ceiling about eighteen feet above the floor. A rough hole about three feet in diameter is in the center of the ceiling. According to tradition, the individual to be imprisoned in this pit was lowered through the hole. Once the rope was pulled back up, escape was impossible. Was this where Jesus, his body marred by the beatings, spent the hours of darkness late that Thursday night and early that Friday morning?

Jesus and Pilate

Jesus and Pilate ■

Locate on your map of Jerusalem the Fortress Antonia. How far did Jesus have to travel in his weakened condition?

If, as tradition suggests, the house of Caiaphas was in the southwest quadrant of the city of Jerusalem, the mob again took Jesus on a long trek through the winding city streets to Pontius Pilate. Most likely, he was in the Fortress Antonia in the northeast quadrant of the city, adjacent to the Temple. This fortress was the center of Roman authority in Judea; it was here that the soldiers were garrisoned; and it was here that Pilate stayed on his infrequent trips to Jerusalem. (Pilate much preferred the Roman seaside city of Caesarea, the city where he and the other procurators or governors lived, to the dry, dusty, crowded city of Jerusalem. Caesarea surrounded these rulers with things Roman; Jerusalem surrounded them with things foreign to them.)

Roman evidence and evidence from the historian Josephus suggests that the procurators usually came to Jerusalem for the Passover and Feast of Unleavened Bread, for these were times ripe for revolution in the Holy City. Crowded as it was with pilgrims, a show of Roman force and presence was necessary to insure order and compliance.

Who Was Pilate?

Who was this man Pontius Pilate? He was the Roman appointed governor or procurator; that we know for certain. Rome had appointed governors of Judea since banishing Archelaus to Gaul in A.D. 6. Pontius Pilate was the fifth in a succession of four-

Bible 301

Who Was Pilate? ☐

In a Bible dictionary, look up Pontius Pilate. How does history remember Pilate? How would the Jewish people have regarded him?

teen governors. He administered Judea from A.D. 26 to 36; his ten years in office were the second longest term of any of the governors appointed by Rome between A.D. 6 and 66, when Rome ceased ruling Judea by governors.

The Gospel accounts tend to picture Pilate as a weak, indecisive person; but this picture is far different from the secular pictures of Pilate recorded by Josephus and Philo. Josephus reports that Pilate offended the Jews when he allowed his troops to bring military standards into the city; these standards bore the image of Caesar. When the Jews protested and offered themselves to be slaughtered by Pilate's troops, the governor backed down. The same historian relates another incident in which Pilate sought to use the Temple treasury to build an aqueduct. Pilate's troops, dressed as civilians, mingled in the crowd of protesters, and at a prearranged signal slaughtered many Jews.

On another occasion, according to Josephus, Pilate ordered an attack on a group of Samaritans who were gathered at Mount Gerizim. Pilate considered their gathering an insurrection when in reality it was a religious ceremony. And Philo reports an incident in which the emperor himself ordered Pilate to remove from his house golden shields bearing the emperor's name. Relations between Pilate and the Jews were not smooth; apparently Pilate had little regard or respect for the faith of the Jews; and as tensions worsened over the years, Pilate was finally ordered to Rome to account for his stewardship of Judea by Vitellius the imperial legate to Syria.

Jesus Before Pilate ■

Read Matthew 27:11-26; Mark 15:2-15; Luke 23:2-5, 13-25; John 18:33-38. What portrait do you see of Pilate in the Scriptures? What regard did Pilate seem to have for the Jews and for their religious observances? How might Jesus have expected to have been treated by Pilate?

Jesus Before Pilate

The encounter between the broken and bloodied Jesus, standing bound before the governor, and Pontius Pilate, sitting on the judgment seat in all his regal finery, challenges the imagination. Yet the four Gospels show remarkable consistency in describing this meeting. In each of the four, Pilate asks Jesus if he is king of the Jews (Matthew 27:11; Mark 15:2; Luke 23:3; John 18:33). Jesus' response in the three Synoptic Gospels is a simple, "You say so" (Matthew 27:11; Mark 15:2; Luke 23:3). His response in John's Gospel is quite similar: "You say that I am a king" (John 18:37).

Does this suggest that Jesus knew full well that no response would release him from the terrible ordeal before him? Affirming that he was king would be a confession of the crimes for which he was unjustly charged; to deny that he was a king would be untrue to God. Perhaps that is why John describes Jesus' answer as: "My kingdom is not from this world" (John 18:36).

But those who delivered Jesus to Pilate continued to badger Pilate for action, hurling charges at Jesus, to which he made no reply (Matthew 27:12-14; Mark 15:3-5). Even Pilate's protest that he found no fault in Jesus did not silence the clamor for blood (Luke 23:4-5).

Give Us Barabbas! ■

Review Matthew 27:15-26; Mark 15:6-15; Luke 23:18-25; John 18:39-40. Ask several volunteers to read aloud one of the Gospel accounts. Have Pilate and a narrator. When the text refers to a response of the crowd,

Give Us Barabbas!

As if to mollify the cries for blood, Pilate reminded the people that his custom was to release a prisoner on the feast day (Matthew 27:15-26; Mark 15:6-15; Luke 23:18-25; John 18:39-40). Consequently, he offered to release for them one Barabbas, variously described as a bandit (John 18:40) and as a murderer and insurrectionist (Mark 15:7; Luke 23:19).

Jesus With Herod ■

Following the lead of those who had delivered Jesus to Pilate, the crowd, perhaps growing larger each moment (for the judgment seat was, according to tradition, in a public area), shouted over and over again that Barabbas be released and that the man Jesus be executed by crucifixion. Even Pilate's entreaties, asking to know what evil Jesus had performed, were met with a clamor for crucifixion. So Pilate gave in to the wishes of the mob; he released the prisoner Barabbas, ordered the brutal flogging or whipping of Jesus, and sent the soldiers out to crucify the man Jesus (Matthew 27:21-26; Mark 15:11-15; Luke 23:18-25; John 19:1).

have everyone else read together, loudly.

How did you feel to be screaming for Jesus' death (or to hear others)? What were you thinking as you participated? How might the disciples and other believers have felt?

Jesus With Herod

Read Luke 23:6-16. Herod was "very glad" to see Jesus because he was hoping to see a sign. What did Herod see before him; how must Jesus have looked?

Several interesting points crop up in the Gospel accounts of these events. One is Luke's account of Jesus' visit with Herod, the Roman ruler of Galilee who happened to be in Jerusalem at the time (Luke 23:6-16). Because Jesus was from Galilee, Pilate sent him to be interviewed by this Herod. Apparently, Herod found no fault in Jesus and sent him back to Pilate.

Herod and his soldiers seemed to have had a kind of "circus" mentality about Jesus: they dressed him up, paraded him around, and sent him back to Pilate. What does this tell you about him as a leader? What does his new-found friendship with Pilate imply, both for the governance by Rome and by local religious and civil authorities?

A curious dimension of this episode is the friendship between two old enemies, Herod and Pilate, that arose from the visit of Jesus to Herod. Why did Luke report this event, but none of the other Gospel writers report it? Absolute reasons are unclear, but Luke admits (Luke 1:1-3) that he gathered all the information he could find about Jesus in order to prepare his Gospel, and quite possibly this was one of the stories that was being told and retold by the time of Luke's writing.

Perhaps Luke included this story to help buttress his case that Pilate was aware of the innocence of Jesus, just as Matthew used the stories of Pilate's wife's dream and the handwashing to demonstrate Pilate's belief that Jesus was without fault. Recall that Luke was writing to a Gentile and largely Roman audience. Did he want to show Pilate in some form of favorable light in order to gain a better hearing among the Romans?

Undercurrents

A second interesting point is the statement in Matthew 27:18 and Mark 15:10 that Pilate was aware of the jealousy the chief priests held for the preacher from Galilee. Just how did the Gospel writers know at this point what was in Pilate's mind? Or might this be a case, as some scholars have suggested, to deflect some of the blame for the execution from the Romans and onto the Jews? Remember that, at the time of the writing of these Gospels, Christianity was struggling for a foothold in the Roman Empire.

A third incident, again reported in only one Gospel (Matthew 27:19), is the warning given to Pilate by Pilate's wife to have nothing to do with Jesus because she, Pilate's wife, had had a dream about Jesus. Pilate's wife is mentioned nowhere else; but on the basis of this incident, she has been declared a saint by the Eastern Orthodox Christian churches.

Yet the reason Matthew inserts this story may be the reason he inserts another story in his Gospel, the handwashing (Matthew 27:24-25). Both of these stories seem to reinforce the point that Matthew wants to make: Pilate believed in the innocence of Jesus. Yet Matthew is writing to Jews; why would he make such a point? Perhaps he did so simply to point out that radical break the Christian must make from the Jewish background. Matthew is trying to convince the Jews that Jesus is the Messiah by pointing out how

Undercurrents ■

What were the undercurrents in this trial as Jesus was passed from one leader to the next? If you were a disciple seeing all this unfold, how would you feel by now?

Privately do some journalling. You can reflect on your own feelings and senses concerning these events or write a letter to any or all of the participants. What would you say to them? What would you want them to know about Jesus? about his relationship to God? to the people? to you? What would you say about their complicity in the Crucifixion? What does all this mean now?

Many people, by their action or inaction, colluded to bring Jesus to trial and to condemnation. Pray for all those who still conspire to damage the work of the faithful church. Consider your own commitment to Jesus Christ and the level of risk you will assume for the sake of the gospel. Take time in prayer to make or to renew your own covenant with Christ.

blind to this fact the Jewish leaders were while even a Gentile like Pilate could see it.

In any case, Jesus had been condemned to be executed by crucifixion; and he was now turned over to the Roman soldiers so that the sentence could be carried out.

Session Six

Crucifixion

Session Focus ■

This session focuses on the crucifixion of Jesus, the physical journey of Jesus to the cross, and the final words he spoke from the cross.

Session Objective ■

You will explore the physical and emotional event of crucifixion to better understand the suffering and sacrifice Jesus made on behalf of humankind.

Session Preparation ■

Have on hand the Gospel parallel, a book of New Testament art, a Bible dictionary, a map of Jerusalem during Jesus' ministry from a Bible atlas or study Bible, copies of your church's hymnal.

Choose from among these activities and discussion starters to plan your lesson.

Crucifixion ■

Read Matthew 27:28-29; Mark 15:16-17, using the Gospel parallel, if you have it. What is the significance

Now the beating and taunting began in earnest. What Jesus had endured in the form of physical abuse at the hands of those at Caiaphas's house was nothing compared with the beatings now leveled on him by the Roman soldiers. Here is where branches of a thorn tree were twisted into a mock crown, then pushed down over the head of Jesus until the blood ran down over his face and neck. Here is where the soldiers spat on him again and again, mocking him, striking him, beating him without mercy.

The Gospel writers do not delve into details. Matthew (27:28) reports that they draped a scarlet robe over the beaten body of Jesus; Mark (15:17) reports that the robe was purple. In both cases, the robe was meant as a jeering taunt at the supposed kingship of the condemned prisoner Jesus.

Even the more apparent inconsistencies between the Synoptic Gospels and John's Gospel are of little import. John reports that the crown of thorns and the abuse by the soldiers took place *before* Pilate handed Jesus over to be crucified; Matthew and Mark report that this took place *after* the accused had been handed over for crucifixion (John 19:1-16; Matthew 27:27-31; Mark 15:16-20). Luke does not mention it.

Visitors to the Antonia Fortress today are shown a stone pavement, the traditional site of the beatings. Scratched into the stones are

of the robe and the crown? How did they become ironic symbols of hope and victory?

If you have a book of religious art, turn to one or more artistic portrayals of Jesus wearing the crown of thorns. How does he look? Does the painting (or other medium) capture the extent of his wounds and fatigue? How does this visual representation affect how you feel about and understand the mocking?

To the Cross ■

Read Matthew 27:32; Mark 15:21; Luke 23:26. Compare these accounts with John 19:17. Why might John's version have departed from the Synoptic versions? What difference, if any, does it make to the community of faith if Jesus did or did not carry his own cross?

Mark and Luke mention that Simon was "coming in from the country," suggesting that Simon was not part of the crowd who knew what was going on and that he had been pressed into service. Does the fact that a stranger helped Jesus, rather than any of the disciples or other faithful men who must have been in the crowd, affect your understanding of the story in any way? Explain.

several marks that are described by tour guides as ancient "game boards" used by the Roman soldiers to determine which soldier had the privilege of abusing the victim first and in what ways. While this is all tradition, it does remind pilgrims of the sadistic nature of some of the Roman soldiers, many of whom were illiterate mercenaries from territories conquered by Rome's armies.

To the Cross

The soldiers had methodically beaten Jesus until his entire body was wracked with pain. Now it was time to go to the place of crucifixion. The Synoptic Gospels use the word *led* (Matthew 27:31; Mark 15:20; Luke 23:26), suggesting that a rope was fastened around the condemned, most probably around his neck, and that he was jerked, dragged, and forced along the streets of the city toward the place of execution.

Several questions arise at this point. Did Jesus carry his own cross to the place of execution? Part of the Roman execution ritual was that the condemned would carry his own cross, or at least the crossbar of the cross, to the place of crucifixion. In some instances, the victim's hands or arms were fastened to the crossbeam of the cross before the trek to the place of execution began. John reports that Jesus carried his own cross to the place of crucifixion (John 19:17). The three Synoptic Gospels indicate that the soldiers forced a bystander, a man named Simon of Cyrene, to carry the cross for Jesus. Cyrene was a region in North Africa; this Simon may have been a Jew in Jerusalem for the Passover, or he may have been a merchant in Jerusalem for the festival. We simply do not know more about Simon, save for some legends that have grown up around him.

Why compel a bystander to carry the cross for Jesus? This was surely not an act of compassion on the part of the soldiers. More likely, Jesus struggled under the burden of the cross, which weighed at least seventy-five pounds, due to the repeated beatings and blood loss. Perhaps the soldiers simply wanted to get on with it and tired of Jesus' inability to move along quickly enough to suit them.

A second question concerns just where the place of execution was. Sources from the Roman period indicate that the Romans always executed criminals in very public places, often busy crossroads, in order to impress on the populace the folly of violating Rome's laws. Despite the hymn, Jesus was not crucified on "a green hill far away"; he was crucified at a very busy intersection or in another very public place where all could see him and shudder at Roman justice. The procession to the cross wound its way through the city streets of Jerusalem, Jesus stumbling, falling, being whipped, the target of insults and objects hurled by bystanders, all the way.

Bible 301 ☐

Look up Simon of Cyrene *and* Cyrene *in a Bible dictionary. Where is Cyrene? What do we learn about Simon and his native land? What does this add to your faith undestanding of the Crucifixion?*

Place of Crucifixion ■

Using the map of Jerusalem, track the distance from the Fortress Antonia outside the city walls to the supposed place of crucifixion, if your map suggests a location. How far did the condemned have to carry the cross? How far could you carry seventy-five to one hundred pounds, even in the best of circumstances?

The Place of Crucifixion

An ancient tradition suggests that the place of execution is now within the Church of the Holy Sepulchre in Jerusalem. This site was identified in the mid-fourth century by the Empress Helena, mother of Constantine, the first Christian emperor of Rome. Another, more modern tradition places the Crucifixion in an area just outside the present city walls at the foot of a rock formation that resembles a skull. This area is known as Gordon's Calvary, after the British archaeologist who identified the site. In reality, the actual site of the Crucifixion has been lost to history. But the

*significant factor about both of these tradition-
al sites is that they are a considerable distance
from the Fortress Antonia where Jesus was
tried and convicted.*

The Stations of the Cross ■

Have you visited the Stations of the Cross in Jerusalem or attended a service that had them depicted in the nave of the church? Describe that experience and what it meant to your faith.

Make simple charts or signs for each of the stations, and place them around your sanctuary. As a devotional exercise, visit each station and pause there to meditate on what that station meant to Jesus and to pray. You may share insights from your time of reflection, but only if you wish to. This is intended primarily as a solitary exercise.

The Stations of the Cross

Long-standing Christian tradition has traced the path of Jesus from the Fortress Antonia to the traditional place of the cross. This path is known as the *Via Dolorosa*, Latin for "painful way." According to tradition, fourteen incidents took place on the way to the cross, and these incidents have come to be known as the "stations of the cross." Many churches, especially Roman Catholic churches, depict these fourteen stations around the interior perimeter of the naves of the churches, and these become focal points for prayer and meditation.

The Via Dolorosa

The fourteen stations of the cross, well marked within the ancient walls of Jerusalem, are traditional; not all are scriptural. This does not mean these incidents did not take place; it means instead that while the Gospel writers did not dwell on the journey to the cross, these things may have taken place.

These are the traditional fourteen stations of the cross. 1: Jesus is sentenced (Luke 23:24); 2: Jesus is given the cross (John 19:17); 3: Jesus stumbles; 4: Jesus meets his mother; 5: Simon is compelled to carry the cross (Mark 15:21); 6: Veronica wipes Jesus' brow with a napkin (Veronica was a bystander who, taking pity on Jesus, wiped the sweat and blood from his brow with a handkerchief.); 7: Jesus falls a second time; 8: Jesus tells the women of Jerusalem not to weep for him but for themselves (Luke 23:28);

9: Jesus falls a third time; 10: Jesus is stripped of his garments (Matthew 27:35); 11: Jesus is nailed to the cross (Luke 23:33); 12: Jesus dies (Luke 23:46); 13: the body of Jesus is taken from the cross (Matthew 27:57-59); and 14: the body is laid in the tomb (Matthew 27:59-60).

At Golgotha

At Golgotha ■

Wherever Golgotha was, it was at or near a public thoroughfare. How has this place been characterized (or even romanticized) in our hymnody?

Imagine that all of our capital crime punishments were carried out at the largest mall in the community or outside at the largest and busiest intersection. Would you stop to watch? Would our society, with its apparent penchant for violence in our visual media, see it as entertainment? How does that image affect your faith understanding of the Crucifixion?

The procession arrived at a place called Golgotha, the place of a skull (Matthew 27:33; Mark 15:22; Luke 23:33; John 19:17); and there Jesus was executed by crucifixion. Crucifixion was not new to the Romans; it had been their favorite form of execution for many years, especially for traitors and insurrectionists, and continued to be the preferred method of execution for many years after the Crucifixion.

In a typical crucifixion, the accused was either tied or nailed by his wrists to a cross. In some cases, this was a T-shaped cross, in others the cross was X-shaped. Our tradition indicates Jesus was crucified on a T-shaped cross in which the vertical part of the T extended above the cross bar. Because of the shortage of wood in Judea, the cross was only high enough so that the feet of the condemned were off the ground. A low cross also gave passersby an easier target for their hurled insults and objects.

The Cross

The Cross ■

How many pieces of "cross" jewelry do you have? What does that jewelry adorn? (earrings, necklace, tie tack, lapel pin) What are they made of? What do they look like? Are they pretty? clean? shiny? expensive? Now think about what a cross used for crucifixion would look like, feel like, smell like. What

The shape of the cross was important for the execution because it stretched the condemned's limbs, especially the arms, at a hideously unnatural angle and forced the arms to carry the primary weight of the body. This weight on the outstretched arms caused immense pressure on the chest and lungs, making breathing labored, difficult, and painful. If the entire weight of the body were suspended from the outstretched arms,

does it mean to you to wear a symbol of filth, torture, and death as a lovely (sanitary) adornment? Would the symbolism carry more power if the adornment looked more like the real thing? Explain.

death would be relatively quick—perhaps in a few hours. But if the body were supported in part by placing the feet on a small shelf or by anchoring the feet to the cross so that the legs could support some of the weight of the body, the death agony would be prolonged considerably.

In some instances, a peg was driven into the cross so that the condemned straddled this peg, again providing some support for the body. The purposes of the shelf for the feet or the peg to be straddled were the same: to prolong suffering, pain, and agony and to prevent a quick and merciful death. The goal of crucifixion was the death of the accused, but the purpose of crucifixion was to cause as much suffering, anguish, and pain as possible before that death took place.

The Wine Drink ■

Read Matthew 27:34; Mark 15:23. What is gall? myrrh? Why might Jesus have refused the drink?

The Wine Drink

The Scriptures report that Jesus was offered wine mixed with myrrh or gall, but he refused to take it (Matthew 27:34; Mark 15:23). This mixture was a mild narcotic, dulling somewhat the agony of the cross. Why did Jesus refuse this mixture? Commentators suggest that Jesus wanted to be fully awake and aware, not drugged or unconscious (and the Gospel writers needed to report Jesus that way).

Taking Jesus' Clothes ■

Read Matthew 27:35; Mark 15:24; Luke 23:34b; John 19:23. This is the second time Jesus lost his clothes, which by now would have been soaked with blood and sweat. What, do you think, would it have been like to see the Son of God in such a condition? Why would someone want those clothes?

Taking Jesus' Clothes

The Romans always crucified criminals naked; it was one more element of total humiliation, total degradation, total vulnerability. It also gave the swarming, biting insects, attracted by the blood, more flesh to torment. The Gospel writers report the soldiers gambling for Jesus' clothes (Matthew 27:35; Mark 15:24; Luke 23:34b; John 19:23); he had been stripped once before while in Pilate's custody (Matthew 27:28).

Find in your book on religious art several renderings of Jesus on the cross. Or, recall any of the more recent movies made of Holy Week events. How is Jesus portrayed on the cross? How "real" is it?

We find it difficult to imagine how it would feel to be crucified. How do you relate to the sacrifice Jesus has made for your sake and for the sake of humankind? What sacrifices are you willing to make for God? What sacrifices might God be calling on you to make?

Sing or read one or more of the hymns about the Crucifixion. How do the music and lyrics help you

Fixed to the Cross

Next, Jesus was attached to the cross. Though some victims were tied to the cross, Jesus was nailed to the cross through his hands (probably his wrists, which was usually the case). Thus, after the Resurrection Jesus showed Thomas his hands (which included his wrists) to convince the doubter that he really was the same crucified Jesus (John 20:24-29). Our imaginations are taxed to the extreme as we picture the broken, bloody body of Jesus being stretched forcibly on the cross; as we hear the sounds of the hammer blows driving the broad, square spikes through the flesh and bones of his hands; and as we see and hear the forced, labored breathing of the victim and see the bruises, the blood, the lash marks covering his body.

Then the cross was set upright. Perhaps it was lifted upright by several soldiers, then dropped into a prepared hole. Or perhaps the vertical timber of the cross was already in place, and the cross bar, victim attached, was hoisted into position.

But the Gospel writers do not dwell on these details. In fact, the Gospel writers report the Crucifixion with a single phrase: "There they crucified him" (John 19:18; variations in Matthew 27:35a; Mark 15:24a; Luke 23:33b). Does this suggest that the process of crucifixion was so well known to the original readers of these Gospels that details were not important? Or did the Gospel writers seek to divert the reader's attention from the man on the cross, as if the scene of the bloodied, bruised, broken, naked man was too much for the Gospel writers—and perhaps too much for us?

So Jesus was crucified, along with two others. The Synoptics report that Jesus was placed in the middle with the crucified "ban-

understand this event? relate to Jesus' sacrifice and suffering? appreciate God's great gift?

dits" on either side of him (Matthew 27:38; Mark 15:27; Luke 23:33, note "criminals" rather than "bandits").

It was nine o'clock Friday morning (Mark 15:25). The sequence of the next incidents is not consistent among the Gospels, but several things took place, perhaps at about the same time.

One, the soldiers divided what small bit of property Jesus had in this life. John reports four soldiers, the Synoptics do not indicate a number. All four Gospels report that the soldiers resorted to casting lots for the garments of Jesus, or at least for the seamless tunic (John 19:23-24). This casting of lots for the earthly possessions of Jesus reminded those who witnessed this incident of Psalm 22:18.

Ridiculing the King ■

Read Matthew 27:37; Mark 15:26; Luke 23:38; John 19:19-22. What did it mean that, according to John's account, the inscription was written in Hebrew, Latin, and Greek? Who would have understood each of those languages? How did God use for the good what was intended for ridicule?

Ridiculing the "King of the Jews"

Two, an inscription was placed on the cross of Jesus, most probably nailed to the cross above his head. The wording of the inscription was plain, direct, unmistakable: It proclaimed Jesus as the King of the Jews (Matthew 27:37; Mark 15:26; Luke 23:38; John 19:19-22). Note in John's Gospel how the posting of the inscription is attributed to Pilate and how Pilate resists the urging of the chief priests to change the wording to "This man said, I am King of the Jews." Again, is John, struggling for Roman acceptance of the Christian faith, attempting to exonerate Pilate just a bit to demonstrate ever so slightly that Pilate really favored Jesus as much as he could, given his official position?

And three, Jesus was subjected to verbal— and quite possibly physical—abuse while on the cross. The victims on the cross were fair game for persons hurling rocks or rotten fruit, garbage, or even offal. This added humiliation was not only tolerated but encouraged by Rome. Passersby engaged in all kinds of mockery, jibes, and catcalls.

The Seven Last Words

The Gospel writers report that Jesus said several things while hanging on the cross, his life slowly ebbing from him as the pain and physical torment increased, though they are pieced together from the four Gospel accounts. Jesus' words from the cross have come to be called the "Seven Last Words." Of some significance here is the number *seven*, often used in biblical narratives as a symbol of completion or totality, for example, the seventh day on which God rested, having completed the creation of the universe in six days (Genesis 2:3).

The First and Second Words

The first word from the cross, according to tradition, was, "Father, forgive them; for they do not know what they are doing" (Luke 23:34). Jesus' first words from the cross were a prayer, and a prayer not for himself but for his tormentors. Some traditions suggest that the "they" to which this prayer refers are the Roman soldiers and/or the religious leaders. Perhaps we can also understand it as prayer for all those who cried for his execution, including us.

The second word from the cross was addressed to an individual, intended to comfort. Luke reports that one of the criminals who was executed alongside Jesus mocked Jesus. But the other criminal silenced the first by reminding him that the two were being justly "rewarded" for their crimes, but that Jesus had done nothing wrong (Luke 23:39-41). Then, in a poignant moment of

The Seven Last Words ■

As you study each of the words, consider asking a volunteer to be ready to read aloud each word, attempting to capture the inflection and intent of Jesus.

The First and Second Words ■

Read Luke 23:34. To whom to you think these words were addressed? How do they inspire you to forgiveness in the most difficult of circumstances?

Read first Matthew 27:38-44; then Mark 15:27-32 and Luke 23:33, 35-42. In Luke's account, even one of the bandits taunted Jesus. Imagine how someone in dreadful pain and suffocating to death would have the presence of mind and the breath to spend that way. How does this add to the humiliation of the event for Jesus? Then read Luke 23:43.

How did Jesus rise above the humiliating events going on around him? What does Jesus model for us? What resources do you have that allow you to rise above insult, injury, or pain?

The Third Word ■

Read John 19:25-27. This is one of the few passages that indicate that any of the disciples were nearby. What would it have been like to be a disciple and to stand by, unable to do (or to prevent) anything? How would you have felt as the disciple into whose care Mary was placed?

Jesus had other male family members who surely must have been in Jerusalem with their mother for the Passover; it is highly unlikely that she would have traveled there alone. Why, do you imagine, would Jesus commend his mother to a disciple? How does his concern for others in the midst of his own tremendous pain influence you?

faith and trust, the second criminal turned toward Jesus and said, "Jesus, remember me when you come into your kingdom." He (Jesus) replied, "Truly I tell you, today you will be with me in Paradise" (Luke 23:42-43). A promise, a dream fulfilled, and an eternity in glory. At the very depths of his suffering, Jesus offered forgiveness and compassion to another who was in the depths not only of physical suffering but spiritual suffering as well.

The Third Word

The love and compassion of Jesus and his concern for others extends to the traditional third word from the cross. This incident, reported in John 19:25b-27, involved Jesus, his mother, and a disciple, often thought to be the apostle John. Even from the cross, Jesus could see those standing nearby. Gazing around, he caught sight of familiar figures. One was his own mother, standing near the cross with two other women, Mary Magdalene and Mary, the wife of Clopas, both of whom were known to Jesus. Standing with the three women was one of Jesus' disciples, one who had deserted him in the olive grove the previous night. Jesus' words were simple, direct, filled with compassion and love: "Woman," he said to his mother, "Here is your son." To the disciple, perhaps John, he said, "Here is your mother." John rose to the occasion and "from that hour the disciple took her into his own home."

Forgiving his abusers. Assuring a penitent bandit. Making permanent accommodations for his mother. Jesus' first acts and words from the cross were acts and words of love reaching out to others, including those who were strangers to him, those who were sinners, and those of his own family.

Jesus had been hanging on the cross for three hours; the sun was now at its zenith; it was high noon. The men on the crosses were in torment. Stinging and biting insects swarmed over their naked bodies. Blood and perspiration dripped from their flesh. Breathing was labored, heavy, difficult, intensely painful.

The Fourth Word ■

Read Matthew 27:46; Mark 15:34, then read Psalm 22 aloud. Notice how many times the psalmist moves from despair to hope (for example, from verses 1-2 to verses 3-4). How would you characterize this psalm overall? How might this psalm have strengthened Jesus during his ordeal? What elements of your worship and devotional life can you tap into when you are in great distress? How do they help you?

The Fourth Word

About noon a strange phenomenon took place. A darkness fell over the whole land (Matthew 27:45; Mark 15:33; Luke 23:44). Here, at what was supposed to be the brightest part of the day, a thick darkness engulfed Jerusalem and its environs. Some commentators have suggested that the darkness was caused by an eclipse, but that would not have been possible, given the full moon at the time of Passover. During this time, the man on the cross was silent. At least from high noon until three o'clock in the afternoon, Jesus made no sound. He hung there in anguished torment, but he was silent.

At about three in the afternoon, Jesus cried with a loud voice in pain and suffering. Those who stood close by could understand his words. He spoke in Aramaic, the language of the day, but his words were the opening words of Psalm 22, an ancient psalm of lament: "My God, my God, why have you forsaken me?" (Matthew 27:46; Mark 15:34).

These words have attracted much speculation over the centuries. Did Jesus feel deserted by God? Was he calling to mind a familiar psalm of lament, as you and I may recall the words of a hymn or a bit of Scripture when we are facing extreme difficulty? Perhaps he completed reciting the psalm in silence. Perhaps he did feel deserted; for as a man, he would have experienced all the pain and despair to which humans are heir.

The Fifth Word ■

Read Matthew 27:48; Mark 15:36; John 19:28-29. Recall the words of Jesus in John 18:11 about drinking of the cup. Then look up Psalm 69:16-21. How was "Scripture fulfilled"? What did this drink symbolize?

The Fifth Word

John (19:28) reports that Jesus simply uttered the very human words, "I am thirsty." In response to these words, several in the crowd put sour wine on a sponge, put the sponge on the end of a stick, and held it to Jesus' lips (Matthew 27:48; Mark 15:36; John 19:29). The sour wine or vinegar was again a mockery of Jesus; it offered him not even an instant's relief from the pain. He who offered the world living water was being offered lifeless water, sour, spoiled wine. Was Peter present in any way? Did he recall Jesus saying, just last evening in the olive grove, "Am I not to drink the cup that the Father has given me?" (John 18:11). Even the simplest acts in the crucifixion of Jesus were filled with symbolism and meaning.

The Sixth and Seventh Words ■

Ask for several volunteers, in turn, to read John 19:30 aloud. Encourage each volunteer to read the verse in a different way to suggest possible ways that it may have been uttered by Jesus. Do the same for the last word, in Luke 23:46. How do the different readings affect the meaning and import? How does each way affect your faithful understanding of this event?

The Sixth and Seventh Words

The traditional sixth word is found only in John 19:30: "It is finished." But how we wish the Gospel writer had indicated the inflection with which Jesus said these words. Were these words of hopeless despair, uttered in a sense of defeat? Or were these three words a cry of triumph, victory, success! Might Jesus have been announcing through these words that he had indeed completed his task, his mission was fulfilled; he had achieved all that God had sent him to accomplish? The ordeal was over; God's will had persevered. Might Matthew's and Mark's accounts, claiming that Jesus gave a loud cry after receiving the sour wine (Matthew 27:50; Mark 15:37), lend some credence to the suggestion that this was indeed a cry of triumph, of accomplishment?

And the last word, found only in Luke 23:46, was again a quotation from a Psalm (Psalm 31:5): "Father, into your hands I commend my spirit."

The Death of Jesus

Read Matthew 27:50-56. What do these dramatic phenomena (the torn curtain, earthquake) mean? What do they symbolize?

The tombs opened and evidently remained open for three days when "bodies of the saints" appeared in Jerusalem (27:52-53). Envision the chaos in Jerusalem for those three days if these events were literally true. Would this have made a believer out of you as it did the centurion?

What would you, as a believer, want to say to the other witnesses after these dramatic happenings?

The Death of Jesus

So Jesus died. Death overtook him and he died. Jesus was dead. He was not in a coma; he was not in some sort of suspended animation; he was not unconscious. Jesus was dead. And for a time, his lifeless, dead body hung there on the cross.

Matthew's awesome words describe what happened next: "At that moment the curtain of the temple was torn in two, from top to bottom. The earth shook, and the rocks were split" (Matthew 27:51). The curtain was that veil that separated human beings from God in the Holy of Holies of the Temple. Now the curtain was torn in two, and humankind could see God face to face. Was the tearing of the curtain symbolic? Was the earthquake symbolic rather than real? The death of Jesus on the criminal's cross forever broke the barrier between humankind and God and effected a reconciliation between God and the people that would last throughout eternity.

But in reality, so moving was the death of Jesus that a centurion, a Roman officer charged with commanding a hundred soldiers, uttered in profound humility, "Truly this man was God's Son!" (Matthew 27:54; Mark 15:39; Luke 23:47, an "innocent" man).

Now the soldiers moved into action at the request of the Judean authorities. The Romans respected the local customs enough to insure that the condemned were dead and that their bodies were removed before the start of the sabbath, at sundown on Friday. They broke the legs of the two bandits, for by breaking the legs the entire weight of the body fell on the arms, further compressing the lungs so that breathing was impossible. The two bandits died quickly. But the soldiers saw that Jesus was already dead; no need to break his legs, just as the regulations for the Passover lamb required that none of its bones should be broken (Exodus 12:46).

The Burial

The Burial ■

Read Matthew 27:57-61; Mark 15:42-47; Luke 23:50-56; John 19:38-42. Jesus was dead. Without the benefit of our hindsight, which celebrates the Resurrection, how might you have been feeling? Now what would you have done? Where would you have found hope?

A man named Joseph, from Arimathea, visited Pilate. He asked for the body of Jesus. Joseph was a secret disciple of Jesus, for he was also a member of the Sanhedrin. Pilate did not care what happened to the body, so with a shrug he gave the body to Joseph. Joseph, with the help of other loving hands, took the body of Jesus down from the cross, anointed it with spices as was the custom, wrapped it in the linen winding sheets of the dead, and placed the body in a new tomb in a garden near where the execution took place (Matthew 27:57-61; Mark 15:42-47; Luke 23:50-56; John 19:38-42).

Jesus was dead. His body was encased in a rock tomb with a rolling stone covering the door and Roman guards posted to insure that no one stole the body (Matthew 27:62-66). This death was real; Jesus was dead.

Closing Prayer ■

The Crucifixion was a particularly brutal event. Collect your thoughts about how you have vicariously experienced the Crucifixion through this session. What did you feel; how did your other senses help you imagine the sights, smells, sounds, tastes, and touch of the guards, crowd, onlookers, and so on?

Pray for Christian martyrs and victims of abuse and cruelty. Consider your own willingness to stick with your Christian values and principles when things get difficult. Take time in prayer to make or renew your commitment to Christ.

Session Seven

Finished—or Begun?

Session Focus ■

This session focuses on the accomplishment of the Crucifixion and Resurrection.

Session Objective ■

You will gain more insight on how Christians have attempted to make meaning from the Crucifixion and have a deeper understanding of the Atonement.

Session Preparation ■

Have on hand the Gospel parallel, copies of your church's hymnal, a Bible dictionary, a book of New Testament art, and a map of Jerusalem during Jesus' ministry from a Bible atlas or study Bible.

Choose from among these activities and discussion starters to plan your lesson.

Finished—or Begun? ■

Read Matthew 27:57-60; Mark 15:42-46; Luke 23:50-54; John 19:38-42. Use the Gospel parallel, if you have one.

Dead. The word cannot be used too often or too bluntly. Jesus was dead. The wine mingled with gall that he tasted just before he died was not a narcotic to give the effect of death while life remained. In no sense was the man Jesus still somehow alive when his body was taken down from the cross. He was not in a coma, nor in some kind of suspended animation, waiting for the right moment to be resuscitated. The man Jesus was dead. His body had been removed from the cross, wrapped temporarily in the winding sheets of the grave, and placed in a new tomb hewn from solid rock (Matthew 27:57-60; Mark 15:42-46; Luke 23:50-54; John 19:38-42).

A huge stone had been rolled in front of the opening to seal the door. Matthew reports that the next day, which would have been the sabbath, some of the chief priests and Pharisees requested that Roman soldiers be ordered to stand guard over the spot lest the followers of Jesus come and steal the body away (Matthew 27:62-66). That a delegation of chief priests would have gone to Pilate on the sabbath and made such a request could be construed as a violation of their own laws forbidding work on the holy day. It may also indicate the lingering fear these men retained about the man Jesus that he might disappear or escape somehow.

In the early centuries of the Christian faith, several heresies (false teachings)

Imagine that you are one of Jesus' disciples or followers. Jesus is dead. How do you feel? What do you remember of what he told you about his death and its aftermath?

Would you be tempted to a kind of docetism? Would that belief hold any credence for you? any comfort? How would you reconcile the belief that Jesus just appeared to be human with your experience?

emerged. Among these heresies were several *docetic* heresies, beliefs that argued that Jesus was too divine to suffer any real pain on the cross. Jesus only appeared to have been a human suffering on the cross, Docetists would argue, and only appeared to have died. Since Jesus was so different from us, his death was different from ours.

But Jesus did suffer as a man, and he died on the cross. He was dead as you and I will one day be dead. Jesus died a very real, very human death.

Who Is to Blame? ■

Several possibilities are mentioned for taking blame. Consider having a panel made up of a representative of each of the groups mentioned who will justify and explain their group's part in the Crucifixion. You may draw on information about these groups that has been presented in this and in previous chapters.

Who Is to Blame?

We twenty-first–century citizens often seek someone or something to blame for those events we consider tragic or unjust. Therefore, perhaps we are not unusual in wanting to blame someone for the crucifixion of Jesus. The act was so horrible, the events leading up to the act were so unjust and unrighteous, the entire situation so out of control, that we want to be able to point the accusing finger of responsibility at someone and thereby begin to wreak our vengeance. So who was to blame for the crucifixion of Jesus?

Roman Soldiers? ■

What do you recall about the character and behavior of the soldiers? Read Matthew 27:27-31; Luke 23:36-37; Mark 15:39.

Have you ever had to do something distasteful, or even wrong, because you were "under orders"? Describe that experience. What did you do about it?

The Roman Soldiers?

Roman soldiers performed the actual crucifixion. They prodded Jesus through the streets of Jerusalem; they forced him onto the cross; they pounded the nails through his hands; and they hoisted the cross to a vertical position so Jesus could die an agonizing death.

But these soldiers were acting under orders. They neither knew nor cared who or what Jesus was. They had not been privy to the late night trial in the house of Caiaphas nor to the encounter between Jesus and

Pilate. Quite possibly, they would not have understood what was transpiring and almost certainly would not have cared what was taking place. They were the execution squad; and when they were directed to perform an execution, they did so with professional dispatch. They can be faulted with the death of Jesus, yes, but perhaps not entirely.

Pontius Pilate?

So what about the Roman authorities, Pilate in particular? Surely Pilate knew when he gave in to the clamor of the crowd exactly what would become of the prisoner. Could Pilate have saved Jesus from death? Of course. Why did he not do so? Perhaps because Pilate was both a realist and a relativist.

He was a realist enough to know and see that he had an angry mob before him and that the city of Jerusalem was swollen with citizens of Judea who could turn that angry mob into a ragtag revolutionary army. And perhaps Pilate was a relativist enough to calculate that saving the life of one man, even though he be innocent, was not worth an armed revolution in which many, many persons—Romans and Judeans alike—could be killed.

Like it or not, we must remember two added factors. One is that during the first century in Roman provinces, life was cheap. Execution was the accepted punishment for many crimes, and execution was always swift, sure, and immediate. The other factor is that the Romans believed that the peoples of the conquered provinces were inferior, second-grade, surely not to be compared with the dignity and value of Roman life.

So the ruthless, bloodthirsty Pontius Pilate turned over to the execution squad this wan-

Pontius Pilate? ■

Review Matthew 27:2-26. Imagine this scene from Pilate's point of view. Why have you been bothered with this petty issue? With the mob getting out of control, what should you do? What are your legal constraints? What does your wife have to say, and what was the effect of listening to her? How did it feel to have the crowd take responsibility for you (Matthew 27:25)?

dering preacher, perhaps wishing that he, Pilate, had never been bothered with such a petty circumstance that had grown to mob proportions. Pilate and the Roman administration of Judea can be faulted with the death of Jesus, but perhaps not entirely.

The Law of Moses?

The Law of Moses? ■

Read Numbers 15:32-36 and Joshua 7, examples of God's wrath against sin. How would the religious authorities know that Jesus had *not* violated the law? What would happen to our legal system if authorities picked and chose which laws to enforce and which to ignore? How would one decide?

How do you define and decide on the authority of religious teaching? What makes a Bible teaching, for example, authoritative for you? How do you reconcile the biblical laws that we routinely ignore (such as food laws, sabbath laws, punishments for certain crimes) with other portions of the Bible that we see as ultimate authority for our lives?

What about the ancient law of Moses? Was the man Jesus guilty of violating that law and deserving of death for that violation? The Hebrew Scriptures tell of persons who were executed for breaking the sabbath or for blasphemy. The anger of God burned brightly against such persons, and their actions very often led to their executions at the hands of the community (see, for example Numbers 15:32-36 and Joshua 7). Could Jesus have been accused of violating the law in such a way that he deserved death?

As with any code of law, the written law must be interpreted by persons facing situations in which the law must be defined, interpreted, and applied. The accusations against Jesus made in Caiaphas's house were accusations of blasphemy—at least to those who heard those accusations. And because it was they who defined and interpreted the law, their judgment prevailed.

Although the Gospels tell us that false accusers were brought to witness against Jesus, even the Scriptures report that some of Jesus' actions could be defined and interpreted as violations of the strict taboos against apostasy. Jesus forgave sin, which according to the Scriptures God alone could do, and equated himself with God the Father (see for example John 5:16-18). The illegality of an action is always in the perceptions of the accusers and those who sit in judgment.

Thus, the ancient law of Israel—or at least

the way that law was interpreted—can be faulted for the execution of Jesus, but not entirely.

The Sanhedrin?

Two other groups are often cited as being responsible for the death of Jesus; and while these two groups played some part, neither can be faulted entirely for the execution of the man from Galilee.

One of these groups was the Sanhedrin, the "supreme court" of Judea at the time of Jesus' arrest and death. While it is true that many of those who gathered in Caiaphas's house that night, and even some of those who accompanied the prisoner Jesus to Pilate, were chief priests and members of the Sanhedrin, no strong evidence suggests that the Sanhedrin sitting in formal session condemned Jesus. It is highly unlikely that the Sanhedrin would have been called into a formal session during the evening of a major feast day. How much more probable it is that some of the members of the Sanhedrin, along with others, either came or were summoned to the house of Caiaphas that night.

How many members of the Sanhedrin were present? No one knows. Did those present constitute a majority or quorum of the Sanhedrin? No one knows. All that can be said with confidence is that *some* of the high priests, *some* of the elders, and *some* of the scribes were arrayed against the man Jesus. These leaders held sway that night and the next morning at the house of Caiaphas, at least enough to have Jesus delivered to Pilate. But to claim that this was a formal action of the Sanhedrin is without convincing evidence.

The Sanhedrin? ■

Consider John 11:45-53; Caiaphas's comment that it was better for one man to die. The context for this remark is earlier in Jesus' ministry than the events of Holy Week. Might Caiaphas have made up his mind much earlier than at this hasty trial? Explain.

How do you deal with a difficult or sensitive situation in which a key player has already determined a course of action in which others need to have a say? What role does your faith play in giving you the courage of your convictions?

"The Jews"?

Certainly the crowd was made up of Jews, although in John's Gospel, at least, "the Jews" refers not to the general population, but to the religious leaders, particularly those who did not accept Jesus as Messiah. How has this accusation against "the Jews" colored your impression of the responsibility of an entire group in Jesus' death? How has it contributed to anti-Semitism in the church?

"The Jews"?

A second group that has been saddled with the responsibility for the death of Jesus is "the Jews." Perhaps more evil has been perpetrated in the name of Christ against Jewish persons than against any other group in the long and often bloody history of the Christian church. Clearly, "the Jews" did not kill Jesus. To say so would be tantamount to saying that either the Jews were unanimous in the decision to kill Jesus or that even a simple majority backed the execution. Neither squares with the facts.

Many Jews supported Jesus. Many Jews cared little one way or the other. Even more Jews, perhaps, had no knowledge of Jesus or what was transpiring in Caiaphas's house or in Pilate's audience room. That some Jews opposed Jesus is accurate. But to blame an entire group of people for what a handful of those people did would be equal to blaming all Americans of all time for the assassination of President John Kennedy. "The Jews" were not responsible for the death of Jesus. Some Jews, some of the chief priests and elders, doubtless had a part in the actions leading up to the execution; but to blame an entire people for the actions of a few is unconscionable.

A Coalition of Forces

If everyone is to blame, is that the same as if no one is to blame? What does this whole issue of blame, fault, responsibility say about God? Why, do you think, would God let the Crucifixion happen? Couldn't salvation and redemption come at a lesser price?

A Coalition of Forces

So who is to blame? As with so many things that take place in our world, no single person or group can be blamed. Jesus was executed by a coalition of forces that converged at the same time in the same place. No single one of these forces would have been sufficient to effect the execution. But a kind of synergy—the whole is greater than the sum of its parts—took place in the garden of Gethsemane, in Caiaphas's house, in

Rather than concentrate on blame, what are the consequences of Jesus' death for his own community? for your community? for you?

Pilate's audience chamber, and on Golgotha. And on this synergy of converging forces can the responsibility for the death of Jesus be placed.

This is not a satisfying answer; we want to blame someone! But this is the only answer that is defensible from the record of the Gospels and from what we know of the history of Judea and Rome. Jesus was executed as both a political and a religious offender; he was executed by *some* Romans due to the actions of *some* of the chief priests and elders of Judea.

Resurrection! ■

Read Matthew 28:1-10; Mark 16:1-8; Luke 24:1-12; John 20:1-18; the accounts of Easter morning. Compare all the accounts. Who was present? Who did what? Who spoke to whom? How did the male disciples discover what had happened?

Imagine yourself in that scene. What would you have thought at seeing the empty tomb? (Remember the fears of the chief priests and Pharisees.) What do you remember of Jesus' words about what would happen to him? How might you have reacted to seeing and speaking to an angel? to experiencing a second earthquake in a few days (according to Matthew)?

Resurrection!

But, praise be to God, the crucifixion of Jesus is not the end of the story! Jesus was sealed in the tomb late Friday afternoon. These preparations were probably carried out in haste, for sundown was approaching and the sabbath would begin, forbidding any work and certainly forbidding contact with a corpse.

The Scriptures simply do not report what transpired on that sabbath day, the day following the execution. Save for Matthew's account of the stationing of the guards at the tomb (Matthew 27:62-66), only Luke makes any reference to the sabbath: "On the sabbath they [the followers of Jesus, especially the women who wanted to anoint the body of Jesus] rested according to the commandment" (Luke 23:56b).

The Jewish sabbath officially ended with sundown on Saturday. But no women would be found on the streets of Jerusalem at night. Indeed, few, if any, persons left their homes after dark; this is why Nicodemus's meeting with Jesus at night (John 3:1-21) is rather unusual.

But the women who wanted to anoint the

body of Jesus did arise well before dawn on the first day of the week, our Sunday, and ran to the tomb through the dark streets of the city (Matthew 28:1; Mark 16:1-2; Luke 24:1; John 20:1). Arriving at the tomb, they discovered that the huge stone had been rolled away from the door and the tomb was empty. Matthew reports a second earthquake (Matthew 28:2; the first being at the time of Jesus' death) and credits an angel with rolling back the stone. The appearance of the angel so filled the guards with fear that they fainted (Matthew 28:4). The other Gospels report only that the women found that the stone had been removed (Mark 16:4; Luke 24:2; John 20:1).

Sing or read together one or more Resurrection hymns. How do they describe the event? How is it theologically possible to celebrate the Resurrection if you have not experienced the Crucifixion and the days of waiting?

The Gospel writers differ slightly in what happened next. The Synoptics describe the encounter between the women and the angel, with the angel reporting that Jesus had been raised from the dead and that they, the women, were to tell all the disciples that Jesus had risen and would meet them in Galilee (Matthew 28:5-7; Mark 16:6-7; Luke 24:5-9). John (20:2-4) indicates that the women raced back to report to Peter and (probably) John, who in turn ran to the tomb and discovered it empty.

Both Matthew and John describe a meeting with Jesus there in the area of the tomb; in Matthew it is Mary Magdalene and "the other Mary" who meet the resurrected Jesus (Matthew 28:9-10), in John (20:11-18) Mary Magdalene meets the risen Christ, but mistakes him at first as a gardener.

Within the unique report of each Gospel is that arguably the greatest single event in all the world's history had just taken place on the first day of the week, the third day after the terrible execution by crucifixion. Christ is risen! Christ is risen indeed!

Why?—and How? ■

What reclaims the Crucifixion from being just one more brutal act? What makes the Crucifixion and Resurrection central to our Christian faith? What does it mean to you to say that Jesus Christ died for your redemption? that God so loved the world that God sacrificed the Son so whoever believes will be saved?

Take a few moments of private time to journal about the Crucifixion-Resurrection event. Reflect on how you participate in it and are gifted by God because of it.

Theories of Atonement ■

These are not the only theories of atonement, and they are very basic descriptions. Consider asking your

Why?—and How?

Perhaps the most perplexing questions of all are "Why?" and "How?" Why was the execution of Jesus necessary? What ends did it accomplish? Could God have accomplished these ends without the brutality of the Crucifixion?

In many ways, the "why" question can be answered rather directly, for we have all experienced that answer. Jesus submitted to execution by crucifixion in order to save us from our sinfulness and to reconcile us to God. In the supreme act of self-sacrifice, Jesus somehow, in some way on that cross, redeemed us and removed our sinfulness, thereby restoring us to a right relationship with God that had been severed by our own self-centeredness.

The resurrection of Jesus the Christ was and is a significant dimension of this act of restoration. Without the Resurrection, the Crucifixion is meaningless—one act of brutality among thousands of similar acts of brutality at that time and since. Without the Crucifixion, the Resurrection is shallow and empty, a case of resuscitation from uncertain death.

But just how do the Crucifixion and Resurrection save us from our sinfulness? How do these events two thousand years ago restore our relationship with God, with a God we have neglected and compromised and often reduced to something less that the awesome holiness that God Almighty demands?

Theories of Atonement

Scholars since the very beginning of the Christian faith have struggled to answer the question of how the Crucifixion and Resurrection save us from our sinfulness. In

pastor to prepare and then visit the group to help explain this complex theological concept.

The Ransom Theory ■

Post two signs at opposite sides of your meeting space. One says "Totally Agree" and the other, "Totally Disagree."

Review the ransom theory, and then take a place near or between the signs that indicates your level of agreement with the theory. Explain why you hold your position.

Consider: Do you believe in Satan as an objective, volitional entity? Is (or was) Satan equal with God?

The Satisfaction Theory ■

Take your place again between the signs to indicate your level of agreement with the satisfaction theory.

Consider: Does God have an honor that can be insulted? that needs satisfaction for wrongs committed? Does God require sacrifices to be appeased? How would we know what pleases or displeases God and what it would take to satisfy? Was Jesus a scape-

trying to answer this question, scholars have forwarded a number of explanations, often called "theories of atonement," to describe how the Crucifixion and Resurrection have brought about our reconciliation with God.

The Ransom Theory

One of the most ancient theories has been called the ransom theory of atonement. This theory, dating back to a couple of centuries after the Resurrection, suggests that the death of Christ was the ransom paid to Satan to purchase our liberation from sin and death. While this explanation held sway for many years, it is based on a belief or perception that Satan had acquired power over humankind in the Fall, at least to the point that God had to pay Satan to release the human souls that Satan held in bondage.

A belief that Satan and God were locked in mortal combat was common in the first centuries of the Christian faith. But as Christian faith continued to develop over the centuries, the belief that Satan was co-equal with God began to fall away.

The Satisfaction Theory

In the eleventh century a new theory was forwarded by Anselm of Canterbury in the British Isles. He suggested that God's very honor had been insulted by human sin and that that honor could only be restored by a "satisfaction" sufficient for God. Human beings alone, being sinful and mortal, could not provide such satisfaction to God's offended honor; only a God-man, that is, Jesus, Son of God, could do so. Because of the sinlessness of Jesus, Jesus did not have to die; because he offered himself to death, the same death we face for our sinfulness, his death provided the extra satisfaction God required.

goat who took on all our sins, who thus traded sins for righteousness (see Leviticus 16:20-23)?

This satisfaction theory is closely akin to another theory often put forward, namely, that Jesus was the blood sacrifice required by the Hebrew Scriptures for the sins of the people. While blood offerings for sin were required in the Torah, assuming that God demanded a blood sacrifice for our sins and a blood offering as a satisfaction for God's offended honor creates some problems. For example, the law of Moses required the people to offer blood sacrifices for sin to appease God. But what kind of appeasement took place when God offered God—the Word become flesh, Jesus the Christ—as appeasement to God's self? Did God appease and satisfy God for what we did?

John Calvin, one of the great Reformers of the sixteenth century, suggested a modification of both the ransom and the satisfaction explanations. Because, said Calvin, Jesus bore for us the "weight of God's vengeance," our sins were imputed to Jesus and Jesus' righteousness became our righteousness. While this seems to be true—we are inheritors of the righteousness of Jesus the Christ, and surely he bore our sins on the cross—was the Crucifixion necessary in order to bring about this reversal, this trading of sins for righteousness? Could not Jesus have taken on our sins and could not we have taken on his righteousness in ways other than by the Crucifixion?

The Moral Influence Theory
The Moral Influence Theory ■

Take your place between the signs and explain your position on the moral influence theory.

Consider: Given human nature, are we moved

Another ancient theory of atonement has been called the "moral influence" theory. It was first put forward by Abelard, a French theologian of the time of Anselm; in fact, Abelard studied with Anselm in the early twelfth century. However, this theory of

enough to change by the example or sacrifice of someone else? Would Jesus' willingness to die for the sake of the good news motivate you to do the same? With so much time and space between the Crucifixion and our historic and social realities, do we actually grieve about and repent because of Jesus' suffering and sacrifice?

Bible 301 ☐

Using a Bible dictionary, look up atonement. What is the biblical basis for it? What is its meaning in a New Testament context?

A Right Relationship ■

What does it mean to you to have a right relationship with God? What do you do to help achieve that relationship? to "keep in touch"?

atonement did not gain much acceptance until the nineteenth and twentieth centuries when it re-emerged with several other concepts during the major shifts in theology that were taking place at the time.

Dissatisfied with the legalities of the other theories of atonement, Abelard suggested that we human beings would be so moved, so conscious stricken, by the crucifixion of Jesus that we would repent of our sins and turn completely toward God. In other words, Jesus becomes the supreme example of obedience and humility, and we are so moved by that example that we seek God's forgiveness and pledge to live only for God. To some extent, Abelard based his idea on the response of the centurion who stood at the foot of the cross of Christ and who recognized in the Crucifixion that Jesus was indeed the Son of God (Matthew 27:54; Mark 15:39).

But was and is Jesus only an example of someone who loved and served God? Is not Jesus Christ far, far more than this? Our world has been filled with persons who have loved and served God even to the point of death and given us example after example to do likewise. If an example of righteousness was all that was required, why could this example not have been set by a mere human being, perhaps an apostle such as Peter or John, both of whom (according to tradition) were executed as martyrs for their faith?

A Right Relationship With God

Perhaps the precise ways in which the Crucifixion and Resurrection of Jesus reconcile us to God despite our sinfulness are beyond our comprehension. Perhaps we cannot explain satisfactorily or at all just how the awful death on a tree saves us from our sinful nature and

Use your journal again to privately write where you feel you are in your relationship with God through Jesus Christ. Where are the weaknesses? the strengths? the concerns? the joys?

Closing Prayer ■

Consider the entire spectrum of Holy Week. What did Jesus do and endure for your sake? How did the general population, the Roman government and representatives, the religious leaders, and the inner circle acquit themselves during this week? Who do you identify with and why?

Use your reflections as a basis for the closing prayer. Lift up to God your new insights and pray for your own weaknesses and failings in your spiritual and faith life. Take time during the prayer to make or renew your commitment to follow the risen Christ.

puts us back into right relationship with God.

We can and do, however, affirm that it does! Each of us who has accepted Jesus Christ as Lord and Savior has also accepted in our hearts and souls (if not always as clearly in our minds) that by his act of obedience to God and his supreme sacrifice even unto death, Jesus Christ has reconciled us to God. He reconciled us and put back together that relationship that we severed by our willful self-centeredness.

The act of Jesus was an act of love, love for us. He knew what God called him to do, but Jesus could have turned back from the cross; he could have summoned legions of angels to save him (Matthew 26:53); he could have, in response to the jeers, saved himself and come down off the cross (Mark 15:31-32). But he didn't. As the old gospel hymn proclaims, "Only his great eternal love made my Savior go." And you and I can no more define and explain the atonement than we can define and explain love, perfect love.